We live in an age that lusts for everything. We want to know more, but we don't want to live what we already know. Orthoscopy will teach you how to discern what is worth knowing which will add clarity to your doing.

—Matthew Kelly,
New York Times best selling author of
The Rhythm of Life

It has been the sincerest of pleasures to get to know Deacon Joe. Among his many admirable traits is his ability to clearly hear a call upon his life and then to have the courage to make it happen. This his first book is again another example of his authenticity. Deacon Joe has chosen the narrow path and shows others how to do the same in this wonderful book. If you are looking to move beyond mediocrity and to follow a call to great service to the Lord and his people, this book is well worth reading.

—Nick Synko, Founder,
Careers Through Faith Ministry,
www.CareersThroughFaith.org

ORTHOSCOPY

*God Bless
Deacon Joe*

ORTHOSCOPY

CLEAR VISION TO SEE WHAT WE OUGHT TO DO
JOSEPH HULWAY

Tate Publishing & *Enterprises*

Orthoscopy
Copyright © 2010 by Joseph Hulway. All rights reserved.

No part of this publication may be reproduced, stored in a retrieval system or transmitted in any way by any means, electronic, mechanical, photocopy, recording or otherwise without the prior permission of the author except as provided by USA copyright law.

Scripture texts in this work are taken from the *New American Bible with Revised New Testament and Revised Psalms* © 1991, 1986, 1970 Confraternity of Christian Doctrine, Washington, D.C.

The opinions expressed by the author are not necessarily those of Tate Publishing, LLC.

Published by Tate Publishing & Enterprises, LLC

127 E. Trade Center Terrace | Mustang, Oklahoma 73064 USA

1.888.361.9473 | www.tatepublishing.com

Tate Publishing is committed to excellence in the publishing industry. The company reflects the philosophy established by the founders, based on Psalm 68:11,
"The Lord gave the word and great was the company of those who published it."

Book design copyright © 2010 by Tate Publishing, LLC. All rights reserved.
Cover & interior design by Leah LeFlore

Published in the United States of America

ISBN: 978-1-61566-839-7
1. RELIGION / General
2. PHILOSOPHY / Religious
10.03.05

DEDICATION

Midway upon the journey of our life
I found myself within a forest dark,
For the straightforward pathway had been lost.
　　　　Dante Alighieri, *Dante's Divine Comedy*
　　　　(As translated by H. W. Longfellow)

This book is dedicated to my wife, Jenni, who interceded on my behalf when I was lost midway upon the journey of my life. She prayed that God would clear my vision so that I might see what I ought to do and not just what I wanted to do.

ACKNOWLEDGMENTS

I would like to thank all those who supported me on this project with their encouragement, especially those who supported me with prayer. A special thanks to those that reviewed a chapter or two and gave me valuable insights on how to make them better.

I would like to acknowledge the staff at the Capuchin Retreat Center in Washington, Michigan. They put up with my almost daily presence in their chapel, where much of this book was written. Special thanks to Father Jogues Constance, OFM Cap., who reviewed this text for me to ensure that it respects the teaching of the Catholic Church. (Sadly, Father Jogues has passed away before this book could be published.)

The inspiration to write this book came to me while attending a *Careers Through Faith* seminar presented by Synko Associates. I would like to acknowledge the encouragement I received from Nick Synko and his team. It was instrumental in my decision to respond to God's call to retire early and to pursue the path of becoming an author.

CONTENTS

INTRODUCTION
13
PURSUING OUR PATH
21
FAITH AND REASON
37
PHILOSOPHY 101
65
LABELS
89
ASKING QUESTIONS
113
WE'RE ALL IN THIS TOGETHER
137

INTRODUCTION

CLOUDS OVER A MOUNTAIN STREAM

There I was, in the Adirondack Mountains, sitting on a rock in the middle of Johns Brook, trying to digest C.S. Lewis's *The Abolition of Man*. The mountains were supposed to be my escape, a short time away from my job, a short time away from my ministry. But now I had let myself become unsettled, not by the realities that Lewis had observed over sixty years ago, but how his prophetic message was clearly being lived out today.

Lewis's short book is only 109 pages long, three chapters and an appendix; just the right size, and weight, for a five-day backpacking adventure. It is small, but it is filled with incredible and timeless observations. The first chapter, "Men without Chests," deals with society's denial of objective values; a desire to build up rational thought at the expense of emotions. Lewis expresses outrage at those that consider themselves to be intellectuals. He writes, "It is not excess of thought but defect of fertile and generous emotion that marks them out. Their heads are no bigger than the ordinary: it is the atrophy of the chest beneath that makes them seem so."

The second chapter, "The Way," addresses the existence of a universal set of moral values that provides a guide for all societies and civilizations; that there are certain things that we *ought* to do and others that we *ought not* do. Lewis refers to this set of values as the *Tao,* and is concerned about its denial by the forces of relativism. He argues, "When all that says 'it is good' has been debunked, what says 'I want' remains."

The final, and title, chapter, "The Abolition of Man," presents the logical conclusion of a society where emotions and values are discredited; where intellect and wants reign supreme. And this conclusion is not only the end of a civilization but the end of humanity. Lewis looks with concern to the past and observes, "I am very doubtful whether history shows us one example of a man who, having stepped outside traditional morality and attained power, has used that power benevolently." He looks to the future, talks about man's attempt to conquer nature, and concludes, "*Human* nature will be the last part of Nature to surrender to Man."

THE CLOUDS DARKEN

I left the mountains and returned home considering how the numerous intellectuals of our time are attacking the moral fabric of our society. I questioned whether our society was becoming more civilized or less. My personal observations of current realities, viewed now in the light of Lewis's arguments, haunted me as I returned to my routine. Are we approaching the abolition of mankind? Are we maybe on an inevitable path in that direction?

Back from the mountains, I returned to my job as an engineer in the automotive industry, an occupation that I no longer found satisfying. It was a good job; I was well compensated. I worked with and for wonderful people, and I was recognized for my accomplishments and contributions. At a time when people were losing their jobs and struggling to survive in the automotive industry, I felt guilty for not being satisfied with a position that many others would envy. But at age 54, I had changed much emotionally and spiritually since those days in engineering school. The industry had changed as well. And the result was that I no longer had any passion for the type of work I was charged with performing. My only source of passion was generated by helping my coworkers, especially the younger ones, to accomplish their project goals and move along, or survive, in their careers.

In an effort to find direction for the next stage of my life, I stumbled upon another book that had a dramatic impact on my life; one that was much more contemporary. And that book was *The Rhythm of Life: Living Every Day with Passion & Purpose,* by Matthew Kelly. Matthew's book gave me great insights into changes I needed to make to be better equipped to face the challenges of life; as he calls it: to be "the-best-version-of-myself." Basically, I was called to restore discipline in my life. As I reflected on my life, I realized it was the discipline that had been present during the most productive periods of my school, work, and spiritual activity. I went charging through the book with an upbeat and positive attitude, filled with the hope that maybe I was on the right track to regaining my balance. But suddenly I came to a halt as I read one of the final chapters of the book entitled "Leaders, Critics, Dreamers, and the Future." Here is the excerpt from that chapter that caught my attention:

> There are five signs of a declining civilization: a dramatic increase in sexual promiscuity; the political undermining and disintegration of family values; the cultural destruction of the family unit; the killing of the innocent; and a radical increase in nonwarfare violence. These signs have played a major role in the decline and collapse of every civilization in recorded history. So much so that once these signs have emerged to some level of general occurrence and acceptance, no civilization

has been able to prolong its existence for longer than one hundred years.

In our own culture, these signs gained initial prominence during and after World War I. They were compounded and spread even more widely by the effects and consequences of World War II, and by the end of the 1960s, they were rampant. At the turn of the millennium, they have all but been generally accepted as valid views and forms of behavior. Therefore, using a date even as late as the 1960s as the landmark for the general emergence of these signs, our civilization is left with only sixty years. This is not a prediction, it is not a prophecy, it is a reality set in the past. It is a lesson we have continually failed to learn from history. And sixty years is a short time for one person, never mind a civilization.

Matthew Kelly, *The Rhythm of Life*

Now I have not researched Kelly's claims regarding the five signs that have heralded the collapse of all previous civilizations. It is clear that all five signs were evident during the fall of the Roman Empire, although the hundred year timeline for its collapse is arguable. We can see the five signs not necessarily as causes of the collapse but as symptoms that the collapse was occurring. Without dwelling on whether these signs have taken place in every declining civilization or whether we have sixty years or a hundred and sixty years left in our civilization, I think we can agree that all five signs currently exist in our society.

And while we may be concerned about the future of our civilization, we must realize that saving our civilization cannot be our goal. As C.S. Lewis puts it in *Mere Christianity:* "We shall never save civilisation as long as civilisation is our main object. We must learn to want something else even more." We must learn to want to do the right things, the things we ought to do and not just the things we want to do. Civilization will take care of itself.

CORRECTING OUR PATH

Is the end of our civilization inevitable? Is it as close as the signs seem to indicate? What can we do now to delay it? What should we be doing now to prevent it? But, most importantly, if our civilization does come to an end, how can we be prepared for what happens next?

These are the questions I pondered. It was my reflections on these questions that lead me to attempt to write this book. My high level conclusion is that our society, our civilization, must once again find its way; it must return to the straight path. It was for this reason that my originally-intended title for this book was *Orthodoxy*. Orthodox means, literally, *correct belief*. Orthodoxy implies traveling a journey along the path that leads in the right direction, and I fear our society is not moving in the right direction today. As I searched the word *orthodoxy* on the Internet, however, I found that there was already a book written with this title. I found that the great G.K. Chesterton had written that book back in 1908, and it was a wonderful find. Like Lewis's *The Abolition of Man*, Chesterton's *Orthodoxy* was a tightly written masterpiece of insights. Every time I read it, I find new meaning and I highlight more sections. I thought at one time of abandoning my own book and directing my efforts to a paraphrased rewrite of this wonderful work, updating it to make its message more accessible to readers of today. I ultimately decided not to do that—yet. That may come later.

SUBMARINES

Chesterton presents an autobiographical explanation of how

he came to know and believe his faith; for him it was Christianity. He takes a much more optimistic view of the state of the world and the ability of civilizations to survive. He did not see that civilization died with the fall of the Roman Empire. For him, it was the existence of faith that provided the light to guide mankind through the darkness so that the civilization could reemerge. This is how he puts it in *Orthodoxy:*

> And in history I found that Christianity, so far from belonging to the Dark Ages, was the one path across the Dark Ages that was not dark. It was the shining bridge connecting two shining civilizations. If anyone says that the faith arose in ignorance and slavery, the answer is simple: it didn't. It arose in the Mediterranean civilization in the full summer of the Roman Empire. The world was swarming with sceptics, and pantheism was as plain as the sun, when Constantine nailed the cross to the mast. It is perfectly true that afterwards the ship sank; but it is far more extraordinary that the ship came up again: repainted and glittering, with the cross still at the top. This is the amazing thing the religion did: it turned a sunken ship into a submarine.
>
> G.K. Chesterton, *Orthodoxy*

Who will be our submarine captains if, or when, our civilization submerges again? Are you ready to do your part to keep humanity on track until it re-surfaces?

ORTHOSCOPY

Since the choice of *orthodoxy* as a title had already been used, I needed to look more closely at the objective of my book and try to discover a new title for my own use. I realized that my objective was not so much to determine or describe the straight path, as it was to look at the obstacles that we all face in finding that path for ourselves and as a society. The real question is: *how can we see more clearly?* Orthoscopic is an adjective meaning *free from visual distortion*. (Not to be confused with the more commonly used word *arthroscopic*, which relates to the inspection of joints.) *Orthoscopy*, therefore, is my noun form of this word and the title I have chosen for this book. I hope to share some reflections that will enable you to have a clearer vision of what you, and society, ought to do.

LIMITATIONS AND QUALIFICATIONS OF THIS BOOK

This book is not intended to change your views or necessarily to try to convince you of the appropriateness of any particular perspective on the issues of our times. At the same time, however, I will make no attempts to hide my own personal views and moral beliefs. To do so would be dishonest and not very workable. I tend to be very transparent and never do a very good job at portraying myself to be something that I am not.

By way of disclosure, I need to share some information about myself and about my faith. I am ordained as a deacon in the Catholic Church. The teachings of the Catholic Church are, for me, my first and foremost guide to finding the correct and straight way through life. This approach is grounded in faith but balanced by the belief that my faith must be reasonable. It is an approach that follows St. Anselm's definition of theology: *faith seeking understanding*. This book is intended for people of all faiths. My hope is that those who do not share my Catholic Christian faith tradition will still be able to benefit from the observations that I share.

This is not a book about religion or about arguing for or against the tenets of any one established religion or denomination. I will use personal examples from my own Catholic faith as illustrations, but not with the intention of proselytizing. This is not a book about religion, but it is a book that presupposes a basic belief in the existence of God. If you truly do not believe in God, then much of this book will be meaningless, and you might want to put it down now and walk away.

In this book, I will often use the issue of abortion as an example to express and clarify some of the points I will try to present. It is clearly one of the most divisive issues of our time and makes a good example for examining different ways of approaching an issue. Since I am a Catholic deacon, it should be already evident what my position is on the issue of abortion. My intention here is not to change your position if it is different than mine, although I admit that this is clearly something I would like to do at another time. No matter what your position is on the abortion issue, I hope you will choose to continue reading this book.

SCOPE

There are three reasons why an individual or society does not travel along the path that is straight. First, there can be a refusal to recognize that a path exists. This subsequently results in a failure to look for it and find it. Second, there can be an inability to see clearly enough to find the path. It becomes lost in the fog and dark. And third, there can be the conscious choice to abandon the path that is clearly identified.

I will touch on the first and last reasons briefly, but the focus of the book is the second reason. This book is addressed to people who want to find the straight path and also want to follow it; people who want to know what they and society ought to do.

PURSUING OUR PATH
(Making Decisions along Our Journey through Life)

On my first business trip to Europe, I traveled with a coworker to Germany. We flew into Frankfurt and then picked up a car to drive to Cologne. We started out okay; we knew where we were, where we wanted to go, and we thought we knew the route to take. But we hadn't traveled very far on the autobahn, the road that we thought would lead us to our destination, when we approached an exit (eine ausfahrt) that indicated a road that led to Cologne. Assuming that this might be a better way to go, we exited onto this two-lane highway and traveled past many intersections and forks in the road, but unfortunately, we did not see any more signs indicating the way to Cologne. The signage on the autobahn apparently indicated all the possible routes, not just the best route. And we found ourselves hopelessly lost.

And so when we saw a familiar Shell gas station, we stopped to ask directions. The proprietor, however, did not speak English, and we did not speak German. So I purchased a map, unfolded it on the counter, raised my hands, shrugged my shoulders, and looked around in the air, and then pointed to the map. The gentleman correctly recognized my gestures to mean *where are we?* and pointed out our current location on the map. I then found Cologne on the map but realized that I didn't know if we should turn right or left out of the station. So I pointed to Cologne on the map and then toward the road and made gestures indicating turning left and right. He shook his head when I pointed to the right and nodded when I pointed to the left. He then went on with his own hand gestures, and more head nodding and shaking, to indicate that we would approach two forks in the road and that on both occasions we should bear to the left. It must have been a pretty comical exchange. Too bad our *discussion* wasn't caught on video.

This experience, however, does point out the importance of knowing where you are and where you want to be. It illustrates that there are many routes to travel, but they are not all equally good. But, most importantly, the story gives us the hope when we feel lost that we can find ourselves again and plot a course to recover our direction.

Do you know where you are, where you are going, and how you are going to get there? If we don't know where we want to go and determine a course to get there, we will never make it to our destination. This applies to each of us individually; it applies to us collectively as a nation and a civilization.

The image of life as a journey is one that I find very helpful. Our world can be seen as a land filled with roads offering us an infinite number of routes that will lead us from Point A to Point B. And every day we have to make choices and decisions about which turns we should make. When we travel the roads, we use maps to guide us; they help us by pointing out restrictions and obstacles that we will encounter along our journey. The knowledge we obtain from our maps gives us the ability to make good choices. We can distinguish the dirt roads from the superhighways and the one-way streets from the boulevards. And we can know the roads that lead to dead ends and the ones that lead us in the wrong direction.

But before we can make any decisions on what paths to take, we have to start with two pieces of information: where we are now, Point A, and where we want to be at the end of the journey, Point B. In your journey through life, do you stop to reflect on where you are and where you want to be at the end of your journey? If so, do you have a course charted to get you safely from here to there? Do our politicians and elected officials consider these same questions for our nation? Or, do they simply look to what will make their constituents happy until the next election?

In our society today, we all become lost at times. But what I find tragic is that there are many who do not even try to pursue and search out the correct or straight path through life. Providing tools and information to remove obstacles so that people can see clearly what they ought to do will make no sense if they don't know or don't care that they are lost. What are some of the reasons for deciding not to even look at the map? Here are a few possibilities why we, or our society in general, might fall into that category:

- We do not stop to consider where we are.
- We do not have a destination in mind.
- We do not believe that a *best* path exists but believe that all paths are equally good.
- We want to live in the dark; we do not want to know the right path because it would take away our spontaneity and may not be the most enjoyable route.

DO YOU KNOW WHERE YOU ARE?

Every man has forgotten who he is. One may

understand the cosmos, but never the ego; the self is more distant than any star. Thou shalt love the Lord thy God; but thou shalt not know thyself. We are all under the same mental calamity; we have all forgotten our names. We have all forgotten what we really are.

G.K. Chesterton, *Orthodoxy*

Perhaps, before we can answer the question, *where am I?* we must first answer the question, *who am I?* But sometimes we get confused and identify ourselves by what we do, rather than by who we are. And when this happens, our identity changes when our activities change, whether by choice or by accident. For example, we hear of many who become lost when their job is eliminated by downsizing. Or maybe it's the football star who loses his identity when he graduates from high school. Maybe it's the woman executive who is afraid to give up her career, her identity, to start a family. Maybe it's the dancer who is crippled in a car accident. We have to search to know who we really are, our unchanging essence.

To find ourselves on the map, we have to know who we are. There are many mechanical engineers located all across the map of the United States, but there is only one Joe Hulway, son of Joseph Hulway and Ann Martony, husband of Jennifer Burgan, and father of Ryann, Cassandra, Brandon, and Andrea. He happens to have worked as a mechanical engineer, ministers as a deacon, makes wine, and hikes in the mountains. When he retired from General Motors and stopped working as an engineer, Joe Hulway's identity didn't change. He didn't go out of existence; he simply changed his activities. Ontologically speaking, he is still the same person.

It is easy to get so caught up in the complexities of life, the everyday effort to make it through one more day, that we focus on *doing* without understanding our *being*. We don't take the time to assess who we really are and where we are on life's journey. We give up control of our life's direction; become followers and not leaders. We may not all be called to be leaders in the general sense of leading other people, but we must all be leaders in the personal sense. We need to take control, leadership, and responsibility for our own lives and actions.

We sometimes accept whatever comes along without seeking what it is that we really want and need. Matthew Kelly refers to this as *surviving* at the sacrifice of *thriving*. Do you know what makes you happy or only what brings you pleasure? What is it that is important to you? How well do you really understand yourself—your strengths and weaknesses? What is your purpose in life? Are there aspects of your current situation that indicate you might be lost and in need of getting back on the right track?

As I hike up and then down the same mountain path, I am always amazed at how different the view appears during the two legs of the journey; it's often hard to believe that I am on the same trail. Coming down the mountain in the afternoon, panoramas are opened up before me between the trees that I didn't see on my way up the mountain in the morning. If I stop and look back, I can regain some of my earlier perspective, but even that is not the same; the sun has shifted to the west painting an image with different shadows than it had before. I'm at the same point in space traveling on the same path, but in the opposite direction, and looking at a different angle and standing at a different point in time. And the world looks much different than it did before.

At any given time, our viewpoint is determined by our location and the direction we are facing as we travel along. Two people can reach the same location from different directions and give two totally different accounts of how the world ahead appears. The same can happen for two people heading in the same direction but at different places on the journey. Our view of life, our knowledge of where we are, is tempered and influenced by many factors, such as our age and maturity, our past experiences, and our traveling companions. Our decisions and choices today may be different than yesterday, because we are no longer in the same place. Our decisions and choices today may be different than someone else's, because we are not in the same place as they are today.

Men are stereotypically accused of being stubborn when it comes to their refusal to stop and ask for directions; we don't want to admit that we are lost, that we don't know where we are. When I'm in my car, I find it easy to fall into this ego trap as well; being lost is merely an inconvenience. But when I'm hiking in the mountains and the consequences of becoming lost are a lot more severe, I am much more prone to stop and take out my guide book, my map, and my compass and determine exactly where I am.

And so it is with our journey through life; the impact of becoming lost on this journey may have eternal consequences. Take some time regularly to stop and assess where you are. Take out your moral compass and spiritual guidebooks and make sure you know where you are now. Find your Point A.

DO YOU KNOW YOUR FINAL DESTINATION?

Anyone who is determined to reach his destination is not deterred by the roughness of the road that leads to it. Nor must we allow the charm of success to seduce us, or we shall be like a foolish traveler who is so distracted by the pleasant meadows through which he is passing that he forgets where he is going.

St. Gregory the Great

Our life's journey is not an endless one. We are merely sojourning here on earth; we are only temporary residents. In the introduction, I mentioned that this book is predicated on a belief in God; that the topics discussed would make no sense without this common thread to connect us together. Our individual religion or faith tradition may impact some of our decisions about what roads we can travel, but our belief in God and the afterlife defines for us our desired ultimate and final destination, our Point B.

Philosophically, we can know that there must be an uncaused cause; the first step responsible for bringing everything else into existence, someone or something that owes its existence to no one or no thing. For most of us, we call that uncaused cause God. Jews, Christians, and Muslims believe that there is only one God, and they call him Yahweh, the Trinity, or Allah, respectively. There can be only one God, but there can be great differences about how we relate to that God, about what we know of his character, attributes, and essence. There can only be one God with a capital G. Those who believe in many gods will usually concede that there is one greater God who was necessary to bring the other gods into existence.

And people who believe in God, and some that don't explicitly, believe that there is a final destination or state to which we aspire. Most of us in the western world call this heaven, but others may call their goal awakening, enlightenment, or nirvana. In any case, there is a reason to take a journey. There is a final destination, a Point B, we hope to reach. Our actions while we are on our journey will determine whether we will arrive there safely.

When we create false gods in our material world, such as

wealth, fame, or power, we automatically create new desired destinations. And creating a new point b (lowercase) is not necessarily bad unless we let it take precedent over our true Point B. For example, if I am driving from Michigan to Florida for a vacation at Disney World, I can decide to take a side trip to visit Mammoth Caves in Kentucky. But it would not be wise to do this if I didn't have enough time and money to accomplish this side trip and still spend the time originally intended with Mickey. And, of course, I cannot let myself get so enraptured with the beauty of Kentucky that I decide to stay and journey no farther.

Be sure in your heart of your final destination; where you truly desire to be when you finish your journey. Give it thought and reflection, and then convict yourself of your choice. When you take ownership for this decision and let it be the star that guides your journey, it will influence your everyday conduct.

DO YOU THINK ALL PATHS ARE EQUALLY GOOD?

> It is better to limp along the way than stride along off the way. For a man who limps along the way, even if he only makes slow progress, comes to the end of the way; but the one who is off the way, the more quickly he runs, the further away is he from his goal.
>
> Thomas Aquinas

If I lived in any major city in Ontario, Canada, and I wanted to travel to a Tim Horton's restaurant for a cup of coffee, I could get in my car and drive in any direction on any road and I would probably arrive at my desired destination within five minutes. It might not make a lot of difference what route I chose, or if I ever planned a route at all; I could expect to find the ubiquitous Tim Horton's without too much trouble.

But going back to my previous example, if I decided that tomorrow I wanted to travel from my home in Michigan (Point A) to Disney World (Point B), this same approach may not be the most practical one. I could get up in the morning, get in my car, and drive in any direction and on whatever road I chose, but it wouldn't be the smartest way to go about trying to reach my goal. I may end the day farther from my destination, not closer. I know that the quickest way and the easiest way for me to get to Disney World is to get onto southbound I-75. I can travel from Michigan to Florida and only need to exit the interstate when I need to eat, purchase fuel, or use the restroom. (Ideally these three needs can be addressed at the same stops, but those traveling with families know that this is not a very likely occurrence.)

Often in our journey through life, however, we are more like the independent driver with a new global positioning system (GPS) navigation device. After he programs in the address of Disney World, he can choose to select the best route based on shortest time or distance and then lock in that route. Once he gets behind the wheel, however, there is nothing to stop our driver from proceeding straight ahead when the voice tells him to turn right at the next intercession. Fortunately, that little voice is very patient and is always willing to recalculate a new route, knowing that once again it too could be ignored. Those new routes will eventually get our driver to Disney World, although possibly via Oregon, but none of them would be as fuel efficient or time efficient as the original.

It is good that we have internal GPS devices that can get us back on track after we have made mistakes in our lives or when we have failed to heed wise direction. But if we think all roads are good and acceptable, we won't know and admit that we are off course. If we don't know that we are off course, we can become hopelessly lost with no chance of getting to our destination before we run out of time or fuel.

GPS navigation devices don't work by magic; they need to be programmed with internal maps and with rules and guidelines for determining the best route. And in just the same way, we have to have maps and rules programmed into our very beings. And these maps and rules need to be consulted every time we reach a major intercession, every time we need to make a decision in our lives. If we don't have any moral maps or moral codes that we believe and trust, it's like turning off or ignoring our GPS unit because all decisions are acceptable. We can turn right or left, continue straight ahead, or just stop for a while and go nowhere at all.

DO YOU WANT TO LIVE IN THE LIGHT?

> And this is the verdict, that the light came into the world, but people preferred darkness to light, because their works were evil. For everyone who does wicked things hates the light and does not come toward the light, so that his works might not be exposed. But whoever lives the truth comes to the light, so that his works may be clearly seen as done in God.
>
> John 3:19–21

When I was a youngster, my parents took me to an amusement park. It was my first exposure to what was referred to as a funhouse. Four of us were loaded into a small car with wheels that swiveled and then launched from our loading platform to go crashing through a set of double doors into the darkness. Once inside the blackness of the funhouse, our thrills began. The small car lurched and made sudden turns. We raced ahead and swerved suddenly as skeletons and monsters popped out of the walls, narrowly avoiding their attacks. We slammed through what appeared to be solid walls. I hardly breathed, and then suddenly we crashed again through another set of double doors, back into the sunlight. My eyes twinkled with delight.

I begged to ride through the funhouse again, and after lunch, I was given my chance. But something happened during this second ride which took all of the fun and excitement out of ever riding this amusement again. Partway through the second ride, our car came to a sudden stop in the darkness. There had been a malfunction of the equipment, and we were stuck. The operators would have to come in to make repairs, and to do so, they turned on all of the lights in the funhouse. With the lights on, I was able to see the pattern of the tracks and all of the mechanisms that triggered the scary effects. And suddenly, the funhouse lost all of its appeal. The ride would never again have the same magic now that I had seen it in the light.

Many go through life trying to stay in the dark so that life will be more fun and exciting. But they fail to see that the path they are traveling leads nowhere, despite all of its exciting turns and adventures. In their chosen world of darkness, they fail to see the path that will lead to true happiness and settle, instead, for one that provides fun and entertainment.

I'm sure you have met individuals or groups that appear to fit this behavioral pattern. If searching out God's will means that they may no longer do as they please, believe what they want to believe, then they make a conscious decision to turn off their GPS unit and remain in the fog without any maps. Obviously, you are not one of these people or you wouldn't be reading this book. But many that we perceive to fit this category don't really fit either. They are simply struggling to know and accept the existence of God; looking for proof that there is a reason to look for a straight path.

THE PRIMROSE PATH

> Do not, as some ungracious pastors do,
> Show me the steep and thorny way to heaven,
> Whiles, like a puff'd and reckless libertine,
> Himself the primrose path of dalliance treads
> And recks not his own rede.
>
> William Shakespeare,
> Ophelia speaking in *Hamlet*

During my first semester in college, I was blessed with one of the most caring and concerned professors I have ever encountered. After almost forty years, I still remember his name—Professor Stonestreet. The class was Calculus II, and he knew how important this subject would be for building a foundation for the rest of our engineering careers.

One morning, Professor Stonestreet went to the chalkboard and, starting with a couple of basic equations, proceeded to fill the entire board with an elaborate derivation. As he got to the end, with the board completely filled with equations, he wrote the final result. To the surprise of all of us sitting in our seats, this final result was obviously incorrect. The good professor turned around and faced us for the first time in almost half an hour and proclaimed, "Gentlemen, you have just let me lead you down the primrose path." One or more of the steps that the professor had made during his derivation was obviously in error. But none of us caught the error, or errors, and we were led astray from the truth.

How important every little step is along the way if we want to find the truth. One misstep can cause us to become hopelessly lost. But a series of correct choices will never get us into trouble.

And so, in a way, I have led you down a bit of a primrose

path in this chapter in emphasizing the need for plotting your course from Point A to Point B, when what is really important is striving to make good decisions at each turn and corner. We listen for our GPS to guide us at each intersection, without being overly concerned with viewing the overall route map. The overall route will change due to circumstances outside our control. We will encounter obstacles that require detours, the map of our world may change, or our circumstances and responsibilities may change such that we now find ourselves in a minivan instead of a sports car. Our ability to identify a course and stick with it, regardless of the circumstances, is not always appropriate. What is important at every moment is that we know where we are, that we remember where we want to be, and that we have good rules to make good choices along the way, keeping these first two pieces of information in mind. Knowing the overall route in advance is not as important as knowing that we are on the path we ought to be on, moving in the direction we ought to be moving, today.

This concept of a path that we should travel is common across faith traditions. Our religions attempt to give us help with finding the right path. In the introduction, I mentioned that C.S. Lewis used the expression *Tao* to describe a universal set of moral codes, and the Chinese character, *Tao*, translates to *the way*. In Christianity, we look for guidance from the teachings of Jesus Christ who we refer to not only as *the way*, but also as *the truth and the life*; for Christians, Jesus is not only the path, but also the destination. In Jewish tradition, there is the *Halakhah*, which translates literally as *the path that one walks*. And in Islam, there is the *Shariah*, which translates literally as *the path to the water source*.

Differences in our beliefs about the nature of God can be the source of great division; our different understandings of the correct way through life can cause us to fight for different choices and decisions in our society. But the commonality of our beliefs in the existence of God can be a great source of unity. There is a wonderful book written by Peter Kreeft entitled *Ecumenical Jihad*. The very title seems to be a contradiction, but Kreeft contends that the common effort of people of faith fighting against the forces of evil will ultimately result in bringing people of different religions together as they fight a holy war against the common enemy.

MOVING ON

This book is intended for the people who have chosen to look for and pursue a path through life by making good choices each day, but who are having trouble finding the straight and narrow path for themselves. The following chapters will hopefully provide assistance by removing some of the obstacles that cloud our vision and prevent us from seeing what we *ought* to do, even if that might not be the thing we *want* to do.

But before we move on, it is probably good for you to set this book down for a while and reflect on the four main questions posed in this chapter. Spend some time in quiet and ask yourself:

- Do I know who I am and where I am now on my journey?
- Do I know clearly, and accept in my heart, what destination(s) I want for my life's journey? (You may have some *hoped for* stops along the way before your final destination.)
- Do I believe that some of my options and choices in life are better than others; that there is a set of best choices in my life that will lead me more directly to true happiness? Am I willing to accept a moral code that will

give me direction on things I ought or ought not do?
- Do I truly want to live in the light and understand the consequences of my decisions, even if it may be inconvenient and take away some of my fun?

FAITH AND REASON
(Why Do We Act Like Teenagers?)

> While we rejoice in the new possibilities open to humanity, we also see the dangers arising from these possibilities and we must ask ourselves how we can overcome them. We will succeed in doing so only if reason and faith come together in a new way, if we overcome the self-imposed limitation of reason to the empirically falsifiable, and if we once more disclose its vast horizons. In this sense theology rightly belongs in the university and within the wide-ranging dialogue of sciences, not merely as a historical discipline and one of the human sciences, but precisely as theology, as inquiry into the rationality of faith.
>
> Pope Benedict XVI, "Faith, Reason and the University: Memories and Reflections"

In his comments at Regensburg in September of 2006, Pope Benedict spoke about the need for both faith and reason and cautioned about the perils to be encountered when either of the two is set apart as the sole source of direction. The Islamic community took great offense at his comments because one of the tenets of their religion was called out as an example of blind faith; an article of faith that was not reasonable. And for this reason, the pope's speech drew wide international attention.

A major portion of Benedict's speech, however, was addressed at the secular humanism of the west; a sort of religion of its own. Secular humanism eschews faith and attempts to rely only on reason. In our western world, there is no longer much acceptance for things of faith. Much of the focus of the speech was against the secular humanists, but they didn't react or respond. They didn't even seem to take notice. They saw the speech only as a further attempt to attack people who failed to use reason.

Our world is quickly losing its faith and its belief in the supernatural, or, if not being lost, they are being compartmentalized and hidden away. Faith is no longer politically correct. And this is one of the reasons why we have such trouble finding the way to truth; we choose to ignore much of what we already know. We pretend that all the knowledge we have obtained through faith is not relevant when we discuss the issues of our time. Every debate is started with a clean sheet of paper as we try to determine the truth using only reason.

It would be quite impossible to grow up this way. As small children, we put our faith in authority figures to show us what is good for us. Our parents, our teachers, and our ministers are seen as trustworthy sources to guide us and supply us with direction for life. We marvel at how much they know and how wise they are. We accept what we are taught without question.

But when we reach adolescence, all of a sudden Mom and Dad don't seem so wise anymore. Although they still know what is good for us, their knowledge of what we ought to do interferes with our desire for what we want to do. All the lessons we learned in Sunday school start to conflict with what we experience as our circle of contacts broadens in high school. We start to question the existence of God and rebel about attending church every week. Instead of faith being a source of comfort and security, it now becomes an obstacle to our pleasure and our desire to do what we want.

And in this way, I believe our culture is very much in its teenage years. It is not necessarily on the verge of collapse; it is maturing and in transition from blind faith to one that is reasonable. It is a time of rebellion and can be one of great danger, depending on the decisions we make during this critical stage of adolescence.

Our religious leaders tell us what we should do, but we object and we deny our faith as a source of direction. Politicians claim that they believe what their religions teach but that they cannot impose their faith beliefs on their constituents. Why not? When they were elected, the people knew, or should have known, what religious faith they subscribed to. The politicians have no qualms about imposing their economic views on those who disagree with them. They have no qualms about imposing national defense views on those constituents that disagree with them. But when it comes to imposing a view of their social and moral beliefs, then suddenly this is a problem. Faith-based knowledge is treated only as personal opinion; and if it offends anyone, then it is politically incorrect and cannot be entered into the debate.

Official Christian, Jewish, and Islamic moral teachings agree on many of the important social and moral issues of today. Judeo-Christian positions are at the heart of our constitution and have always been the starting point for developing legislation; but not any longer. We are not allowed in our polite political discussion to reference that these religious positions even exist. We argue that bringing a faith perspective to the debate somehow violates separation of church and state; that we may offend someone who claims not to believe in God.

We try to forget that living in a democracy means that we have the freedom to be wrong. If 95 percent of the people believe that God exists, why are we so concerned about the 5 percent of the people who we believe to be wrong on this issue? There is a much greater percentage of our population that believes in the existence of God than believes in manmade global warming, yet our legislators deny God and treat global warming as gospel.

Is the reason that we deny the teachings of our faith truly because we don't want to impose our beliefs on others? I don't think this is always the case. I think it is often because we don't want to impose them on ourselves. We use others as an excuse to allow us to do what we want, rather than what we ought.

ON LOGIC PUZZLES

I don't play very many games, although I do enjoy a daily crossword puzzle. Because my knowledge base is relatively limited, and my memory is not the best, I choose a relatively simple puzzle on the Internet and then challenge myself to see how fast I can complete it, if at all. With crossword puzzles, if I don't know the answers to enough of the clues, I will never solve the puzzle, no matter how long I work at it. But when I finally give up, I can look up the answers and turn my failure into a learning experience.

Sudoku puzzles can also be fun, but after a while, the logic process involved can become very tedious. I know I can eventually find the answer; it's just a matter of how much time and effort I want to expend getting there. With time always at a premium, I would rather not waste it in this way. Crossword puzzles test how much you know and how you can think creatively. Sudoku, and most of the other math puzzles, test how well you think logically and also how much time and patience you are willing to expend.

Another category of puzzles is the logic puzzle, and I think they may be useful for illustrating the interaction of faith and reason. This type of puzzle usually involves several lists of items or characteristics that need to be linked together based on a limited series of clues. It might be a simple problem where there are five houses in a row and five workers—say an engineer, a firefighter, a postal worker, an x-ray technician, and a tool maker. We need to determine which worker lives in each house. There are 120 possible solutions to this puzzle. The first clue might be: "the firefighter lives in a house to the right of the tool maker." From this one clue, we can conclude that the firefighter cannot live in the house on the far left and the tool maker cannot live in the house on the far right. This one clue quickly cuts the number of possible solutions to seventy-eight. What if the clue was instead: "the firefighter lives in *the* house to the right of the tool maker"? Then the number of solutions would be cut to twenty-four. It's amazing how much we can learn from small bits of information.

We could eventually determine which house belonged to each worker by analyzing additional clues. Fewer clues are required to match three workers to three houses; there are only six possible combinations. Many more are required to match ten workers to ten homes; there are 3,628,800 possible combinations. Most of the puzzles, however, add complexity not by increasing the number of items to match but by adding additional qualifiers. We might have to determine the name of the person associated with each occupation and also the color of each house. Adding these two requirements to our original puzzle raises the possible combinations from 120 to 1,728,000.

Some of the keys to this class of puzzles are that there are always enough clues to determine the proper order of the items, there is only one right answer, and the clues don't contradict each other. If only life were so simple. The number of issues that we need to put in order in our lives and in our world is much greater than any logic puzzle. We don't have all the clues we need, and the ones we do have are certainly not laid out in a nice, orderly list.

And this is where our faith comes in. This is where we can count on truths that have been revealed to us by God, usually through our particular faith tradition. Instead of trying from scratch to search for clues to determine what God is like and what He wants us to do, we can accept in faith a hypothesis given to us by our parents and ministers. Then we can test our hypothesis every day to see if it is consistent with the clues we encounter along our journey through life. In a way, it's like working the puzzle backward. If our clues are consistent with our starting hypothesis, this does not prove that our faith is correct, it simply means that it is plausible. When we have checked the consistency of our hypothesis against enough clues, we might conclude that our faith is indeed quite reasonable.

AN EXAMPLE PUZZLE

Here is the first logic puzzle I have ever produced. Although it is not a very creative one, hopefully it will serve to illustrate some important points.

> Three brothers (Bob, Tom, and Andy) and their two sisters (Patty and Sandy) all live on JoAnn Street, a short street that is only four houses long. Four of the siblings live on one side of the street in houses numbered 101, 103, 105, and 107, and the other lives across the street at 104 JoAnn. Number 101 is at the west end of the street. All the siblings have different occupations (x-ray technician, firefighter, tool maker, postal worker, and engineer) and live in different color houses (brown, red, blue, yellow, and white). From the following information, determine where the brothers and sisters live, their occupations, and the color of each house.

- The engineer lives directly east of the blue house.
- One of the sisters is a postal worker.
- Sandy lives in a blue house.
- Tom, the man in the red house, and the x-ray technician all live on the same side of the street.
- Sandy does not live on a corner and lives on the opposite side of the street from her sister.
- The firefighter, who doesn't live in a yellow or brown house, lives on the opposite end of the street from one of his brothers, who lives in a red house.
- Andy lives in a yellow house between one of his brothers and one of his sisters.
- One of the brothers, who is not a tool maker, lives in a white house.
- The tool maker, who is not Tom, lives east of the firefighter.

Now, suppose I handed you an envelope and told you it contained the solution to this logic puzzle. You open the envelope and find the following table printed on a slip of paper:

TABLE 1

Address	Occupation	Name	House Color
101	Fire Fighter	Tom	White
103	X-Ray Technician	Sandy	Blue
104	Postal Worker	Patty	Brown
105	Engineer	Andy	Yellow
107	Tool Maker	Bob	Red

You can choose one of three options:

1. You can put your faith in me and believe that I am trustworthy and have given you the right solution.

2. You can discredit me, finding me unworthy of your trust, and then throw away the envelope and start from scratch to determine the solution by methodically checking the puzzle clues.
3. You can have faith in my solution but still check the validity of the answer to make sure it is consistent with the clues given as part of the puzzle. (I'm sure that many of you have done this already.)

Option 1, the Child Approach: This is faith alone, or blind faith. It is the faith exhibited by a small child learning his alphabet or his multiplication tables. It is also the kind of faith exhibited by many radical fundamentalists of all religions and by cult members. It can be a quick way to gain information but can be a very dangerous approach when people act without any effort to understand if the information they have obtained is reasonable.

Option 2, the Teenager Approach: This option denies faith and depends on reason alone. It is much like the behavior of a teenager receiving information from his parents. It is also the process which currently dominates our political process and can lead to inaction and frustration, as all the different considerations become difficult to comprehend simultaneously.

Considering our puzzle, we could solve it the way a conventional computer program might, by iterating through all 1,728,000 possibilities to find the one that is correct. This may be good for a computer but is pretty difficult to do with pencil and paper. Instead, most attack logic puzzles using a grid like the one shown in Figure 1.

FIGURE 1

		House Number					Name					House Color				
		101	103	104	105	107	Patty	Bob	Sandy	Tom	Andy	Brown	Red	Blue	Yellow	White
Occupation	X-Ray Tech															
	Firefighter															
	Tool Maker															
	Postal Worker															
	Engineer															
House Color	Brown															
	Red															
	Blue															
	Yellow															
	White															
Name	Patty															
	Bob															
	Sandy															
	Tom															
	Andy															

Considering our first clue, it informs us that the engineer does not live in a blue house, does not live in houses 101 or 104, and houses 104 and 107 cannot be blue. This would allow us to places Xs in the boxes that are not possible, as shown in Figure 2. With each clue, more Xs can be placed on the grid until the solution is determined. It is very tedious process; some think it is fun.

FIGURE 2

		House Number					Name					House Color				
		101	103	104	105	107	Patty	Bob	Sandy	Tom	Andy	Brown	Red	Blue	Yellow	White
Occupation	X-Ray Tech															
	Firefighter															
	Tool Maker															
	Postal Worker															
	Engineer	X		X										X		
House Color	Brown															
	Red															
	Blue			X		X										
	Yellow															
	White															
Name	Patty															
	Bob															
	Sandy															
	Tom															
	Andy															

Option 3, the Adult Approach: This option combines the best characteristics of the other two. I propose that it is the most practical and reasonable option, an appropriate adult response. It is the quickest way to reach an answer that can be verified as a rational solution. But we still need to be careful.

Suppose I gave envelopes to two other people and they each contained a slip of paper, one with Table 2 and one with Table 3:

TABLE 2

Address	Occupation	Name	House Color
101	Fire Fighter	Tom	White
103	Tool Maker	Andy	Yellow
104	Postal Worker	Patty	Brown
105	X-Ray Technician	Sandy	Blue
107	Engineer	Bob	Red

TABLE 3

Address	Occupation	Name	House Color
101	Fire Fighter	Tom	White
103	X-Ray Technician	Andy	Yellow
104	Postal Worker	Patty	Brown
105	Tool Maker	Sandy	Blue
107	Engineer	Bob	Red

If these two people also applied Option 3, they would find that their solutions also were consistent with the data available. (In my presentation of the puzzle, there was not enough information supplied to rule out any of the three solutions presented.) But, if the three of you all believed that you had the correct solution, rather than simply a possible solution, that's when arguments and conflicts could quickly arise.

What could the three of you do next? Once again, you could act like children, teenagers, or adults.

- You could act like children on the playground and all argue stubbornly in faith, but without reason, that you each have the correct answer. The exchange might go something like this:
"You're wrong!"
"Am not!"
"Are too!"
- All or some of you could walk away and lose any faith in your answer because it is not unique and lose any interest in finding the true solution because it is too difficult. The teenager might use the slang expression, "Whatever."
- Or you could act like adults and recognize how many points of the three solutions are in agreement with each other. You could work together to find a little more information in an attempt to resolve the minor differences. This option makes a lot of sense, but it is rarely what we choose to do in society. We either fight fiercely for a position based on the world as we see it or we give up on finding the right position and decide that all of them are equally acceptable.

DIFFERENT STARTING POINTS

In life, it is good to begin with a starting point grounded in faith. It is good to test the direction given to us by our faith tradition, or some other trusted source, to see if it's consistent with the reality around us. But we must remember that we will still have disagreements with others because none of us have all the same facts and data available to us. Or maybe we start with conflicting information or assumptions because of differences in background or culture.

For example, in our puzzle, it is a good assumption that the odd-numbered houses are in numerical order and that house number 104 is not on the corner, but this is never explicitly stated. We come to this conclusion based on our knowledge and experience about how house numbers are typically ordered. Or someone given this same puzzle fifty years ago may have jumped to the conclusion that the three brothers were the engineer, firefighter, and tool maker because these were occupations that women would not be expected to pursue at that time.

Similarly, when we deal with issues in our society, we bring different perspectives and viewpoints based on our faith tradition, our culture, and our experiences. It is possible that all the perspectives might be wrong. But it is not possible that all differing perspectives are completely right. They are the starting positions we bring to the table, just like the three people with differing solutions to the logic puzzle. And we have the same three options on how to proceed.

ARGUING WITHOUT REASON

One approach is to assume in faith that we have the correct solution and understanding to a given issue. Confident in our solution, we argue for acceptance of our position but feel no compulsion to back up our arguments with facts and reason. Victory, when following this model, goes to the one who is the strongest, most persistent, or loudest, or to the one who has the solution that is most satisfying to those we are trying to convince. In this process, there is never any intent to determine the right, or even best, solution; we think we already know it. Obviously, this does not appear to be a productive mode of action. It seems rather childish. Unfortunately, it is a process that is all too prevalent in the current arena of partisan politics.

If you have spent any time watching our politicians debate an issue, you realize the truth, and the sadness, of this situation. The typical politician is bent on advancing his own agenda and keeping his constituency satisfied so that he can get reelected or attain higher political office. It is often hard to see how they have the best interest of the country at stake. There is very rarely any evidence that they are pursuing the truth so that they can select the best solution to the problems of our country. Besides, the right solution might be unpopular with their voting base; it is best not to find it.

NO ARGUING, NO REASON

In the face of conflict, another approach is to abandon any hope of finding the correct solution. Sometimes this is done out of a fear of facing conflict. How often we see this in personal relationships of friends and loved ones. It can result when one of the individuals involved has no confidence in their ability to discuss and communicate. It can result when one of the individuals is overbearing and not willing to allow discussion of viewpoints other than his own. Many marriages suffer ongoing problems and disagreements that never get resolved because it is safer to ignore the issues or it is not possible for open discussion to take place.

But sometimes we can take this approach so that we don't appear judgmental. We don't want to criticize someone else's opinion and suggest that they are wrong. We are more concerned that everyone is happy rather than with determining the truth. I ran across an interesting quote that illustrates where this behavior can lead us.

> You taught me to be nice, so nice that now I am so full of niceness, I have no sense of right and wrong, no outrage, no passion.
> Garrison Keillor

But more often we abandon our search for the correct path because it is simply more convenient. Without sure knowledge of the truth, and with our faith position shaken by the possibility of alternative positions, we can be tempted to conveniently choose the one we like the best. It seems rather adolescent; anything goes.

In the automotive industry, the stylists who design the appearance of cars and trucks are not given the freedom to generate any shape they choose. They must follow design criteria so that the vehicle will ultimately be able to be manufactured, shipped, and meet government and performance requirements. I was involved with exterior plastic components during most of my years at General Motors; and at one point in time, the stylists would receive multiple lists of requirements for a component, such as a bumper fascia. One list came from the group responsible for molding the fascia, one from the group concerned with painting it, and others from those involved with areas, such as bumper impact, lighting regulations, or serviceability. Unfortunately, when all these individual lists were compared, there were many points of conflict. And this reality delighted the stylists. Knowing that they could not possibly meet all the requirements given them, they felt free to choose the ones they liked and shape the clay the way they preferred. It took a concerted, multi-disciplinary effort to resolve this issue through centralization of design guides and design best practices.

This approach of convenient ignorance is often used with the issue of contraception. As a deacon, I have the opportunity to meet with engaged couples as they prepare for marriage. I explain to them the Catholic Church's position against contraception and try to explain the beauty of natural family planning (NFP) as an acceptable means for regulating births, if necessary, as part of responsible parenthood. I also occasionally cover this topic in my homilies as a reminder to those who should know the Catholic faith but who have trouble accepting this component and need a little prodding and reminding.

The response that I receive from most of the couples is that NFP is too difficult and would cause stress in their marriages. But when I ask these same couples if they have ever taken an NFP class to learn the truth about how these methods strengthen and enrich the love between spouses, about how little sacrifice is really involved, the answer is always *no*. The Catholic Church tells them that contraception is morally wrong. This should be their faith starting point. But the world tells them that contraception is a good thing. They have conflicting information, so they feel free to do what they want. They are afraid to read the short encyclical, "Humanae Vitae," from Pope Paul VI which speaks clearly to the sanctity of marriage and the dangers of contraception. They are afraid to take an NFP class. If they found the truth, they may feel obliged to follow it.

DISCUSSION WITH REASON

The most appropriate approach to pursue when faced with conflicting resolutions of an issue is to have a logical debate and discussion to try to obtain the truth. This requires that the parties representing both sides of the issue allow themselves to be vulnerable; one position, or both positions, may be proven wrong in the process. It requires that all parties subordinate their egos in the search for the truth. And this is a very difficult thing to let happen, especially in the world of politics where reputations and appearances are so important. It is no wonder that we seldom, if ever, see true debate as part of our political process.

And so if we can't expect our politicians to provide us with the truth, where can we turn. I suggest, for the major divisive topics of our time, that we turn to our faith leaders rather than our political leaders. But our society is reluctant to trust religious authority. I found this quote an interesting one for reflection:

> The modern critics of religious authority are like men who should attack the police without ever having heard of burglars. For there is a great and possible peril to the human mind: a peril as practical as burglary. Against it religious authority was reared, rightly or wrongly, as a barrier. And against it something certainly must be reared as a barrier, if our race is to avoid ruin.
> G.K. Chesterton, *Orthodoxy*

If we choose to look to religious authority for guidance, we must first accept that we want to know the truth and be willing to unify behind it. If that happened, the politicians would have no choice but to follow. They could no longer pretend to be leaders.

ABORTION EXAMPLE: FAITH VERSUS REASON

Controversy regarding the acceptability of abortion is a major divisive issue facing our country today. In the light of our previous discussion, let us look at some of the approaches we apply to the abortion issue in the face of significant differences of opinion.

Arguing without reason: There are some who simply use intimidation to argue for their position, without resorting to reason. It is often a fight for dollars, which in turn buy votes to get a politician who is sympathetic to the cause elected. It is sometimes a matter of who can lobby the hardest or speak the loudest through media campaigns. There are rallies for those who support and oppose the right to abortion which are aimed at changing public and political opinion by a show of numerical support.

No arguing, no reason: This is the approach used by many who call themselves pro-choice. They want to let everyone decide for themselves, all viewpoints are equally valid. Sometimes this approach is taken out of compassion because an individual knows of a friend or relative who has had an abortion. To express an opinion against abortion would be perceived as being judgmental; it's safer not to participate in the debate. And others choose this approach because it provides convenient ignorance. Politicians, for example, can try to avoid taking a stand. Catholic politicians can say, "I support the Church's teachings against abortion, but I cannot impose my views on my constituency," and then vote against legislation which would limit something they claim to condemn.

Discussion with reason: The question behind all the controversy and heated arguments is simply whether abortion is morally acceptable or not acceptable; is it the killing of an innocent human life or not? Justice Blackmun in his majority opinion written for the Supreme Court decision in the infamous Roe v. Wade abortion ruling stated:

> Texas urges that, apart from the Fourteenth Amendment, life begins at conception and is present throughout pregnancy, and that, therefore, the State has a compelling interest in protecting that life from and after conception. We need not resolve the difficult question of when life begins. When those trained in the respective disciplines of medicine, philosophy, and theology are unable to arrive at any consensus, the judiciary, at this point in the development of man's knowledge, is not in a position to speculate as to the answer.
>
> Justice Harry Blackmun

The Supreme Court ruling hinged on one very important missing piece of information: the point at which human life begins. Over the last thirty-five years, how much of the debate and effort has been focused on resolving this core question? Very little, I am afraid. Many seem to be content with the first two modes of dealing with the issue. The Supreme Court decided that it was not their responsibility to decide the question of when life begins and seemed to defer to the consensus of doctors, philosophers, and theologians if that could be achieved. There are some in congress who are now trying to pass legislation to identify that life begins at conception. But I have little confidence that this issue will be resolved on the floor of congress because of the political risks involved.

Who are the best people to give us moral direction on this issue? I suggest it is our priests, our ministers, our rabbis, and our imams. But between Christianity, Judaism, and Islam, there is not even agreement about when life begins. All believe that abortion is wrong, but not all agree that it is specifically considered *murder* at all stages of pregnancy. And so different limitations are proposed and justified.

As I have already mentioned, I am a Catholic Christian. The Catholic Church has a very clear position on abortion. It has not changed over the last two thousand years, but the understanding has developed and matured based on inputs from scientists, philosophers, and theologians. This position is stated in the Catechism of the Catholic Church:

> Human life must be respected and protected absolutely from the moment of conception. From the first moment of his existence, a human being must be recognized as having the rights of a person—among which is the inviolable right of every innocent being to life. Since the first century the Church has affirmed the moral evil of every pro-

cured abortion. This teaching has not changed and remains unchangeable. Direct abortion, that is to say, abortion willed either as an end or a means, is gravely contrary to the moral law... The inalienable right to life of every innocent human individual is a constitutive element of a civil society and its legislation. Since it must be treated from conception as a person, the embryo must be defended in its integrity, cared for, and healed, as far as possible, like any other human being.
Catechism of the Catholic Church, 2270, 71, 73, 74

In the light of these statements, it is difficult to see how Catholic politicians can say that they support Church teaching and still be pro-choice. It appears hypocritical.

As I indicated, however, other major religions differ regarding when human life begins. Judaism agrees that life begins at conception, but that a living being does not receive a soul and does not become fully human until birth. Islam chooses the date 120 days after conception. And of course, our Supreme Court, who admitted that they couldn't be expected to know, arbitrarily chose a date of ninety days after conception before which abortion could take place without any justification.

Are we having the discussions and debates about when human life begins? Do we know more scientifically now than we did in 1973 about fetal development; about when hearts beat and when pain is felt? Can theologians resolve nuances in their understanding of what it means for life to be human? Is it possible that an appropriate team could be pulled together to see if consensus can be reached on this significant open issue from Roe v. Wade? It seems like the adult thing to do.

And there is another underlying question. If we are not sure when life begins, what is the prudent course of action to take until we know for sure? I'll touch on this issue in the next chapter.

WHOM DO YOU TRUST?

So far I have concentrated our discussion of faith and reason on how they are applied, or not applied, to major political issues in our society. And I believe this is important for us because I think we need to all bring our faith knowledge to the public debate about what is best for our country—about what our country ought to do, not just what it can or wants to do. But it is also important because many of our problems and decisions on a personal level are influenced by the shadow imposed by the greater society.

My children and grandchildren are growing up in a society which is much different than the one that existed in my youth. When I was young, there was consistency in the message I heard in church, the one I heard from society, and the one expressed by our laws. Living together without being married was wrong. Abortion was wrong. Homosexuality was wrong. But now, while my church continues to preach that all these things are still wrong (as she has preached for the last 2,000 years), my society and its laws now say that they are acceptable. There is no longer agreement between what is morally acceptable, what is socially acceptable, and what is legal. Children now receive conflicting information and are then told to follow their own conscience.

And following our conscience is a good thing to do, but our consciences must be properly formed. Too often we keep our consciences conveniently ignorant to allow ourselves the permission to do what we want, without ever trying to determine what it is that we ought to do. And so in all the things we do in our lives, we need to find people we can trust to help us structure our belief system and guide our decisions. By ourselves, we are much too prone to rationalization.

We need to develop good starting positions. But the question becomes one of where we place our faith when determining these positions. Whom should we trust?

When I first moved into our home back in 1978, the only equipment I had available to mow about one-and-a-half acres of lawn was a well-used lawn mower my father had loaned to me. It worked well, but with a twenty-inch cut and no self-propulsion, cutting the grass was a day-long, exhausting task. I knew I needed to purchase a lawn tractor but didn't have a lot of time to shop around for the best value. Well, it just so happened that a coworker was also in the market for a lawn tractor. Don initiated a search for the best deal, and each day I would hear about the results of his investigations from the previous evening. Finally, he came in one morning declaring that he had made his purchase the night before. It was a model left over from the previous season; this provided a significant price reduction. It was also the last model from this manufacturer to have an engine with cast iron sleeves; all the new models had all-aluminum engines and would not be expected to be as durable. When he found this value, he immediately purchased one of the two remaining tractors on the showroom floor. And after he finished recounting the details of his buying experience, I picked up the phone and purchased the other one.

Don was a good friend, and I trusted in his honesty. I knew that he had nothing to gain by trying to convince me to purchase a tractor from the same location. And I also knew that he was technically competent and had done his homework during his selection process. For these three reasons, I could put my faith in his recommendation. I could make my decision without doing all the research myself, because I had someone I could trust to help me make that decision.

We need different people in our lives to help us make good decisions in the various areas of our lives. While I trusted Don's input on selecting a lawn tractor, he is probably not the one I would go to for career direction, financial planning, or advice on marital problems. And so, in choosing someone to give us guidance on a specific issue, I think we can look at the same three considerations that I used when I trusted Don's recommendation on the tractor. We can ask the same three questions.

1. Is the person honest and trustworthy?
2. Is the person objective, or does he have a self interest in the decision?
3. Is the person knowledgeable about the subject matter?

Honesty: It is important to choose guides for our life that care about the truth. A desire to search for the truth is a great indicator of a person's character but is a trait that sometimes takes time to become evident. Take your time to get to know someone before you give him your trust; it needs to be earned.

I have often been inclined to take the opposite approach; to trust people until they give me a reason not to do so. It hasn't always worked out very well. This approach may be okay for the non-critical decisions but not appropriate for the really big choices in life.

Lack of bias: We need to understand the motives of those we consider trusting to make sure there are no potential conflicts of interest that might influence their judgment. An otherwise honest person can be tempted to shade the truth for their own benefit.

Are oil executives the ones to be trusted with developing our country's energy policy? Can Planned Parenthood be considered a reputable source of information on the abortion issue when much of their income is derived from providing abortions?

Knowledge: Honesty and lack of bias are not sufficient however. The desire to search for the truth does not ensure the ability to find it. Someone may have our best interest at heart but may not be qualified to give us advice. They may be well-meaning yet steer us in the completely wrong direction. I know many priests that I trust to give me spiritual guidance, but I wouldn't necessarily ask them for advice on how to repair my car. Before we trust someone, we need to make a judgment about their competence regarding the subject matter at hand.

THOUGHTS ON CHOOSING ROLE MODELS AND MENTORS

I joined the Knights of Columbus, a Catholic men's fraternal organization, when I was in my late twenties. Many of the members of our small council at the time were old enough to be my father, some my grandfather. As I attended the funeral of another one of these fine men recently, I paused and reflected on how much I had subtly learned from them early in my life.

These men were farmers, auto mechanics, and well drillers. They were simple, honest men who loved their families—and they were all happy. I learned more about how to be truly happy from their example than from that of most of my contemporaries at work or school. When it came to knowing important secrets of life, these men were definitely competent and worthy of my trust.

We're often most comfortable around people like ourselves. We can have fun with them, but they are probably the ones who have the least to teach us, especially about being happy; they're still learning themselves. Look for role models and mentors in your life who are honest and caring and who have demonstrated that they know things about life that you still need to learn. And then trust them, learn from them, and be at peace.

Our parents are often those people, once we relearn how wise they truly are; we already know about their honesty and caring. But sometimes we need others as well; maybe it is a financial counselor, a career coach, or a spiritual director. Find someone who will guide you to what you ought to do, not just tell you what you want to hear.

For example, trust the real estate agent who encourages you to delay your home purchase until you can put 20 percent down and make payments of no more than 25 percent of your take-home income on a fixed rate mortgage, even if this means the potential loss of a sale. Do not trust the agent who tries to talk you into a zero-down, adjustable-rate mortgage just to get a commission. That sales person does not have your interest at heart.

THOUGHTS ON CHOOSING POLITICIANS

Drew Westen is a clinical, personal, and political psychologist who advises democratic candidates and the Democratic Party on the proper ways to present their message. He has recently written a book, *The Political Brain: The Role of Emotion in Deciding the Fate of the Nation,* in which he laments that voters do not act objectively when they cast their vote for one candidate or the other. He concludes from his research that, "The political brain is an emotional brain. It is not a dispassionate calculating machine, objectively searching for the right facts, figures, and policies to make a reasoned decision."

Westen claims that Democrats have traditionally appealed to voters using facts and data to argue for the rationality of their position on a given issue, while Republicans have been more successful by appealing to their feelings and emotions. He observes that the Democrats often came across as intellectuals. It reminded me a bit of Lewis's concept of men without chests, which I mentioned in the introduction: "It is not excess of thought but defect of fertile and generous emotion that marks them out. Their heads are no bigger than the ordinary: it is the atrophy of the chest beneath that makes them seem so."

Westen uses the example of a Pennsylvania coal miner voting in the 2004 presidential election to illustrate a lack of dispassionate thinking, about voting illogically. The candidates are John Kerry and George Bush. He argues that Kerry is the favorable candidate on the issues most important to our coal miner: working conditions, job security, and the solvency of the social security system. But our miner was more likely to vote for Bush, who was strongest against terrorism, against violent crime, and for family values. From Westen's perspective, "Given that he lives in rural Pennsylvania, he doesn't need to worry much about terrorist attacks or violent crime from inner-city gang members." He also wonders why he would be concerned about "the specter of two men kissing on the courthouse steps in San Francisco."

Fortunately, voters do not necessarily vote for the candidate that promises to meet their immediate, selfish needs. This is a fact to be celebrated, not lamented. Of course, voters don't ignore the candidate's positions that will make their life personally better, that will provide them with things that they want. But they also consider values and principles and reflect on whether the candidate is willing to do the right thing for society, what he ought to do for the good of the country.

How do we decide which politicians get our vote? It can be the cause of much internal tension. Do we vote for the candidate that we want or the one we know we ought to vote for? Many of the specific issues will change in the four-year period after we vote. Do we vote for someone who appears to have good answers to today's problems? Or do we look for someone who shares our values (or who has values), even if we disagree on specific policies? Is this someone we can better trust to face the unforeseen issues of the future?

Personally, I vote for a candidate I can trust, making that determination using similar criteria as discussed earlier.

Honesty: Do we sometimes ignore a politician's track record of dishonesty because they promise policies that meet some personal need or desire of our own? Some argue that it's better having a crook working for you than against you. But remember, if they have lied to others, they will probably also lie to you.

Do we understand how a politician develops his policies? Are they based on a firmly-rooted faith and belief system, a desire to find and embrace the truth? Or are they based on the latest polls and surveys of what the voters want to hear? When they change positions, can you tell if it is because they have advanced in understanding or because they need to change positions to get more votes to get elected?

I am more attracted to a candidate that believes strongly in the truth of his position, even if it disagrees with my position, than someone who has a position in agreement with mine, but only because it is politically expedient. The former, I can hope, will engage in honest debate. The latter can change his mind two days after election for no legitimate reason.

Motivation: What causes a politician to run for public office? I'm sure for most it is a healthy balance of a desire to serve the public, a desire for power, and a desire to feed their ego. But what happens when motivations get out of balance, when personal gain interferes with decision making, or when power and ego become such strong forces that the desire to serve the public interest is compromised or abandoned?

These are difficult questions to answer, especially when our only information comes from short campaign ads on the radio or television. All ads will say that the other candidate is biased and motivated by special interest groups while theirs is not. It takes effort to try to find the truth, to see if the politician's claims are consistent with the facts. We should not cynically assume that all politicians are alike, that they are all in it for themselves. We can examine the candidate's history to see if they have been willing to risk personal and political attacks rather than change their position.

Knowledge and competency: One of the methods often enacted to resolve concerns with the self-interests of politicians is the use of term limits. Unfortunately, while this has some merit, it can also impact the ability to retain public servants with experience and accumulated knowledge of the intricate public policy issues.

We need elected officials who are intelligent and competent, who know the details of both sides of the current issues, and who also know how to work within the current political system to successfully enact legislation. It is often helpful to also have someone in office who has experience outside of political circles to bring a broader perspective and fresh thoughts to the arena of ideas.

SUMMARY

Faith and reason are both important to our ability to make good choices, to determine what we ought to do, but faith comes first. Find people and organizations that you can trust and let them help develop your starting positions, your first drafts, of how you should respond to issues in your life and in our society.

Check these positions against the realities of the world you experience to ensure that they are consistent, that your faith positions are reasonable. When conflicts arise, as is sure to happen, focus your attention on the discrepant areas to determine the facts and data necessary for resolution. Be confident in what you believe and why you believe it. This will help clear your vision to see what you ought to do and help you resist the temptation to simply do what you want to do.

PHILOSOPHY 101
(How to Be Reasonable)

I still have a coffee mug that I received from one of my daughters almost twenty years ago. It has stick figures of a boy and a girl playing. The boy is standing on a wagon flying a kite, and the girl has a yo-yo in one hand and a pinwheel in the other. And the caption on the mug is: "You sure don't look your age . . . but aren't you in about the twenty-fifth grade?" My daughter gave me that mug one Father's Day because she thought it was funny that a thirty-six-year old father of four would go back to school to get another engineering degree. She was amused that we could go to the library on Saturday and work on our homework together.

I think she also found it amusing that seven years later I went back to school once again. This time, it was a spiritual call to become a deacon that led me to the seminary. And for my first class there, I found myself sitting in a classroom preparing to study philosophy. It wasn't something I wanted to do, but it was a necessary prerequisite if I wanted to pursue my diaconate training at the graduate level.

Formal training in philosophy had not been a component of my technical education path in engineering. As evidenced by the mug that I received from my daughter, my lack of prior philosophical coursework was not due to a lack of time spent in the classroom. I had spent five years obtaining my Bachelor of Mechanical Engineering and Master of Science in Chemical Engineering degrees right after high school. Then, after working thirteen years in the automotive industry, my employer sent me back to school for another three years to earn a PhD in mechanical engineering. I was a doctor of philosophy (that's what PhD means) and yet knew nothing formally about practicing the art of philosophy. And so, four years after becoming a doctor of philosophy, after a conversion experience that changed the life of our family dramatically, I walked kicking and screaming into my first philosophy class with a group of seminarians who were half my age.

I was very much in the infancy of my faith, but you could never have told me that at the time. I did not know what I did not know; I was not very wise at all. My faith was very strong, and I didn't see why I had to waste my time having it questioned and put to the test. I had not yet been exposed to the wisdom of St. Anselm's definition of theology as *faith seeking understanding*. I did not yet appreciate that theology was essentially philosophy applied to matters of God and religion. It was right for me to start with faith, but this was not a place to stop. It was now the time to pursue understanding, but I had not yet come to that realization.

I didn't want to be in that philosophy class, and this soon became clearly evident to the wise and holy Monsignor Allen Vigneron (now Archbishop Vigneron) who had the task of guiding us to a love of wisdom that semester. Fortunately, he was very gentle with me and I survived. I not only survived, but I also developed a great love and appreciation for *doing* philosophy. I must admit that I have never gone back and expanded on my formal philosophical education, but I do see things now from a different perspective. That semester I acquired some basic tools to help me be a more rational being. That class was probably the most life-changing one I have ever taken.

In our search for truth, we use our God-given rationality to examine our faith, to determine if our faith is reasonable. Faith allows us to propose a hypothesis, and reason allows us to test that hypothesis. But do we know how to reason, how to be rational? Being rational sounds easy, but it actually takes a great amount of discipline. It can be an arduous task; one that we too often avoid and do not do at all or take short cuts and do not do well.

Being rational is a process rather than a state of existence. And this process of being a rational being I will use as my working definition for philosophy. Philosophy is not something we learn, it is something we learn to do. In this way, it is very similar to my career in engineering; we didn't learn *about* engineering, we learned how to *do* engineering. I must admit that the first time I heard the expression *doing philosophy*, it seemed a little awkward. But I have become more comfortable with this understanding. Our word *philosopher* comes from the Greek words *philos*, meaning lover, and *sophia*, meaning wisdom; a philosopher is one who loves and pursues wisdom. It implies a search that is ongoing, one that will never end unless we could possibly come to know and understand all things. The great philosopher Socrates contrasted himself with the sophists; those who thought themselves to be wise. The sophists did not really love wisdom; they merely wanted to attain enough of it so that they could use it for their own personal gain. And since they thought themselves to be wise, their journey was over. Socrates, however, believed that the only people who are truly wise are those who do not think themselves to be wise. These are the people that continue in the pursuit of truth. This apparent contradiction has come to be known as *Socratic irony*.

Unlike the animals, God has made humans as rational beings. A rational being is capable of pursuing wisdom and truth, and conversely, the ability to pursue wisdom and truth defines a rational being. It is part of the definition of a human being. So again, my definition of philosophy is simply the process of being a rational being. If we are not being rational, we are not being fully human.

It is my opinion that basic training in philosophically-sound reasoning is very much lacking in our education system and in our culture. This is not a claim that I have researched extensively with facts and figures; it is my opinion, based on personal experience and from observation of many young people at work, school, and church. Exposure to philosophy in our schools is often missing or distorted by the trendy concepts from modernity. Young people hear the quaint and abstract expressions such as Descartes,' "I think therefore I am," and they think they know about philosophy. Other than the philosophy majors, those that take philosophy classes at all are usually exposed to concepts of noted philosophers but not how to *do* philosophy.

Archbishop Vigneron gave me a good foundation. I would like to share four concepts that have stuck with me over the years since that first semester at the seminary:

1. Distinctions
2. Categories
3. Causes
4. Reasoned speech versus rhetoric

Archbishop Vigneron will probably be disappointed that this is all I remember. (I was surprised when I pulled out my old class notes how much more I should have learned. It's always bad when we forget things that we have learned; it is worse when we forget that we ever learned them in the first place.) It is my intention to communicate at least these four topics in an understandable way and not disappoint the good bishop even further.

DISTINCTIONS

Our efforts to have rational debates are often doomed to failure before we ever get started. We fail to resolve an issue because of how we start out framing the question at hand. We set up a discussion comparing two different possibilities but don't stop to realize that both, or neither, may be correct. And this is what happens when we base our discussions on differences rather than distinctions.

This was, for me, the most practical concept presented in my philosophy class and something I put to use often in everyday life. We were taught to look at distinctions rather than opposites or differences. A distinction establishes a binary condition where one of the two options must be true and the other must be false; like a switch that is either on or off. This condition ensures that the question can be resolved properly. For example, we can ask if something is black or white. If it is actually green, then we can't answer the question. If, however, we ask if something is black or not black, then there is a definite answer, as long as we have an adequate definition of what is meant by black.

In the early days of the Christian church, a very noted controversy arose that demonstrates the need for properly setting up distinctions rather than differences. There were two separate camps, one in Alexandria arguing for the divinity of Jesus and the other in Antioch arguing for the humanity of Jesus. Many heresies arose as these two groups struggled to decide whether Christ was human or divine. They failed for some time to realize that there were two separate questions, not one: *Was Jesus human or not human?* and *Was Jesus divine or not divine?* When the debate was viewed and approached as two separate distinctions, the church could determine that Christ was both truly God and truly man.

At one point, one of my daughters was struggling with making a choice between two young suitors. She liked them both very much and was trying to decide if she should date Tom or Harry. I suggested to her that she was being premature, that before she could decide between Tom and Harry she first had to decide if either one met her requirements for an eventual spouse. (I prescribe to the belief that dating is like an extended job interview for selecting the right person for the position of life-long companion. It makes no sense to call someone back for a second interview if they do not possess the minimum requirements for the job.)

It was really two separate starting questions. It wasn't the question of difference: *Tom or Harry?* It was two questions of distinction: *Tom or not Tom?* and *Harry or not Harry?* I recommended that she first sit down and make a list of the things she was looking for in a mate. There would be some characteristics that were non-negotiable and others that were nice but not necessary. She could then compare the two men in her life against her requirements. If only one met the non-negotiable portion of her list, then the decision of who to date was clear. If neither met that list, then it was time to move on and find someone new altogether. Only if both met the requirements would there be any real decision to be made. She then could move to the nice but not necessary part of her list to see who might be the one to bring her greater happiness.

This mistake of comparing differences instead of distinctions becomes very evident when we look at how the lines are often drawn in the abortion debate. People will ask if you favor protecting the mother's rights or the baby's (usually referred to as the fetus) rights. The abortion question, when framed in this form, will never be resolved. One of the pro-life slogans addresses this misguided line of questioning. It states: "Mother and baby, why can't we love them both?" It reminds us that there are two questions: *Do our actions show that we have love and compassion for the mother? Do our actions show that we have love and compassion for the unborn child?*

There are a lot of questions based on distinctions that can be logically approached on the abortion issue. For example: *Is the fetus human or not human?* Many questions are imbedded within each other and lead to more questions rather than easy answers. Each question must be answered calmly and rationally before any headway will be made in healing the wounds of division between the pro-life and pro-choice camps. It will take much work to attain any real progress, but the promise is that progress can be made. Political appeals that stir emotions and rally support are easy; logical thinking requires hard work. And this hard work is philosophy.

Only when we know with certainty that the fetus is not a human person can we condone and support abortion. If we know with certainty that the fetus is a human person, then we are obligated to do everything we can to stop abortion, because it is clearly murder.

But what if we admit that we do not know with certainty; what then is the prudent thing to do until we have done our philosophy and determined whether the living fetus within the mother's womb is a human person or not a human person? Let's not kill it for sure, just in case it is a human person. Aborting the fetus is totally irresponsible if we have any doubt about whether or not it is a human person. During the 2008 election campaign, President Obama was asked his opinion on when human life begins. He replied that the answer to that question was above his pay grade, and that is a fair enough answer. If he had not taken the time and effort to rationally consider the question and come to his own conclusion, then it was better to admit that he didn't know than to claim an answer someone had prepared for him. But once he admitted that he did not know when life begins, he is then required to protect the fetus in the womb because it *might* be a human person.

If a hunter hears a rustling in the trees but is not sure if it is a deer or a fellow hunter, it is not prudent for him to fire his rifle in that direction. He must first be sure that it is not another person. Here is a perspective from Ronald Reagan:

> What, then, is the real issue? I have often said that when we talk about abortion, we are talking about two lives—the life of the mother and the life of the unborn child. Why else do we call a pregnant woman a mother? I have also said that anyone who doesn't feel sure whether we are talking about a second human life should clearly give life the benefit of the doubt. If you don't know whether a body is alive or dead, you would never bury it. I think this consideration itself should be enough for all of us to insist on protecting the unborn.
>
> Ronald Reagan,
> *Abortion and the Conscience of the Nation*

CATEGORIES

As mentioned earlier, when I attended that first philosophy class, I was no stranger to the classroom or to applying academic principles in my career as an engineer. I had learned much about the principles of physics and had put them to work solving engineering problems. There are certain universal rules and concepts that apply, such as Newton's Laws of Motion and the conservation of energy and momentum. There were structured approaches to problem solving and determining the truth about how things interact in the physical world.

But in philosophy class, I found a different understanding

of the word *physics,* one that was broader and more universal. Physics, in the sense developed by Aristotle, had different sets of rules and structure which could be applied to a better understanding of the natural world. This physics is also called *natural philosophy.* Analogous to traditional physics, it includes its own three principles of motion, or change, and provides a structure that can be applied to the analysis of non-engineering problems. Part of this structure consists of a system of categories.

Aristotle examined words and simple expressions and divided them into ten different categories. The main category is called *substance.* This category contains words that we would expect as the subject of a sentence: i.e., man, tree, bed, or dog. The other nine categories are called *accidents.* The word *accident* in this context is different than our usual English usage. In this philosophical case, accidents describe the state of a substance. They are conditions of the substance that are not necessary for the substance to exist. The accident *blue* may describe a house, but a house doesn't have to be blue to be a house. The accidents are words that provide information about the substance and could be used as predicates to a sentence. Aristotle's nine accident categories are:

1. quantity
2. quality
3. relation
4. place
5. time
6. position
7. possession
8. acting
9. being acted upon

All of the words and expressions that fall into these categories are neither true nor false in themselves; they are simply words. Only when they are combined into sentences, or composites, can they be tested for truth.

If we diagrammed a simple form of one of these sentences, it would look like this: *[Substance] | is \ [accident]*. We simply insert a word or expression from the substance category as the subject of the sentence and a word or expression from one of the accident categories as the predicate. An example might be: *The bread is being toasted*, or *Joe is forty pounds heavier than in college*. These combinations of substances and accidents are statements which we can test for their truth. Essentially, they provide us with the basis for a distinction. Is the bread being toasted or not being toasted?

We know about motion of objects and particles in conventional physics. In Aristotle's physics, he defines motion as a generation of one mode of being coming into being from another mode of being. He proposes three principles of change for a substance coming into being. They are called the matter, the form, and the privation; or the *which*, the *to which*, and the *from which*. It sounds a little abstract at first, but don't get all tangled up with the words. Let's look at a simple example to get a better feel of Aristotle's concept of motion.

If I spend some time out in the sun, my skin will become tan. The *matter*, or the *which*, for this change is my skin. Tanned skin is the *form*, or the *to which*. And pale skin is the *privation*, or the *from which*. I move from being a pale person, one mode of being, to a tan person, another mode of being.

And the ten categories provide ten different ways for a substance to come into being, either substantially or nine ways accidentally. In a substantial change, the matter of one or more substances is changed to a new substance. In an accidental change, the substance is the same before and after the change, it is the matter of the change.

The example of pale skin becoming tan skin represents an accidental change. The substance is the same skin, both before and after the change; it just has slightly different properties or accidents. The same is true for our previous example of bread becoming toasted bread or skinny Joe becoming fat Joe. But if we start with the matter of water and flour and yeast and combine them to make bread, then we have an example of a substantial change; the matter is the same before and after, but a new substance is created.

One application of this concept of substantial and accidental changes is to investigate the beginning of a human life. There is an obvious *substantial* change that takes place at fertilization, commonly referred to as conception. Two separate substances, a sperm and an egg, unite to form a unique new substance, a human zygote. This zygote is called an embryo when it becomes implanted in the uterus, and some use this point as their definition of when conception takes place. (It is important to agree on definitions before we start serious discussions and debates.) And then the embryo is arbitrarily called a fetus twelve weeks after conception. It undergoes many changes before it leaves the womb. The philosophical question is whether any of these changes are substantial or whether they are all accidental changes. What are the differences between a zygote, an embryo, a fetus, an unborn child, and a born child? Are these differences substantial or accidental? The development is continual. Is there anything substantially different from one hour to the next or from one day to the next? Is there something substantial that takes place between the seventh day of week twelve and the first day of week thirteen, or from one minute before delivery to one minute after?

One of the accident categories listed earlier was that of position. Apparently, there are some that are confused and consider a change in position to be a substantial change. These are the people who support the barbaric procedure referred to as partial-birth abortion. To them, as long as the head of the *fetus* is still within its mother, then it is not yet a human child, and they believe it does not have any right to life. They take great pains to prevent the baby from being completely delivered, and they take steps to ensure that it is delivered in the breech position. In this way, the *fetus*, which is 75 percent outside of the mother's body, is not technically a *baby* by their definition because the head has not yet been delivered. This allows them to rationalize that the process of inserting instruments into the skull of the fetus and sucking out its brain is not infanticide. They don't want to look at the situation in rational, philosophical terms. Fortunately, this abortion technique has now been made illegal, but many of our current politicians, intelligent and educated men and women, including our president, Barack Obama, supported the morality of this procedure. Are they confused about the truth or do they want to stay conveniently ignorant of this erroneous technicality so that they can keep a certain portion of their constituency placated? Bread doesn't suddenly become bread when you open the oven door and move the loaf to the counter to cool.

CAUSES

In Aristotelian physics, there is also a series of four *causes* that all changeable beings are said to possess. The word *cause*, in this philosophical sense, is a little different than its current common usage. Causes, in a philosophical sense, are essentially the answers to four questions we might ask to understand a certain thing. And those four questions are:

1. What is it made of?
2. What is it?
3. Who made it?

4. Why was it made?

The four causes are named, respectively, the material cause, the formal cause, the efficient cause, and the final cause. The causes provide us with a structured method of observing the world around us and help us to examine what things are and what they are supposed to do.

Material cause: The material cause answers the question: *What is it made of?* It describes the material or matter from which an object or being is created. For example, the material cause of a statue may be bronze, or the material cause of a chair may be the oak lumber from which it is constructed. The lumber is not a chair, but it has the potential to be formed into a chair.

Formal cause: The formal cause describes the essence of the being or thing and answers the question: *What is it?* It is its pattern or formula. The formal cause describes what it means to be a statue or a chair or a house or a cow or a human being. When the lumber is combined with the form, or essence, of a chair, its potential is actualized; it comes into existence as an actual specific chair. In other words, *what a chair is* becomes *that a chair is.*

Efficient cause: The efficient cause answers the question: *Who made it?* It describes the forces that brought the object or being into existence. For the statue, its efficient cause would be the sculptor; for a child, its efficient cause would be his parents; and for a house, its efficient cause would be the contractor and construction crew. Each efficient cause, in turn, has to have its own efficient cause that brought it into existence; things can't bring themselves into existence. There is, therefore, an infinite line of causality that runs backward in time. And at the end of that line, there must be some initial cause that got everything started, the *uncaused cause.* Some people refer to him as God.

Final cause: The final cause answers the question: *Why was it made?* It is the purpose of an object or being. Sometimes we called it the *good* of that being or object. The final cause refers to the reason for which the object was brought into existence. We often wonder why mosquitoes, or other insects that we consider to be pests, exist. We have to stand back a great distance, sometimes, to see their purpose and their role in the food chain to understand why it is good that they *do* exist, to understand their *raison d'être*.

The formal cause and the final cause are probably the most interesting, challenging, and useful for us to discuss, especially when we think of them in combination. When we try to identify something's purpose, its final cause, we must first identify what that thing is, its formal cause.

A cow can change, but it cannot change into a horse. We look at Old Bessie and know that she is a cow. But what are her general characteristics that tell us that she is a cow, a member of the bovidae family of the bos taurus species? What is it exactly that makes up her *cowness?* If Bessie whinnied like a horse, she would still be a cow, but we might say that her behavior was deviant; it is not what cows are supposed to do. She would not fully meet and fulfill the formal and final cause for a cow.

Everyone knows by experience about trees; we have all seen trees. But we might stop and consider what it is that makes a tree a tree; what gives it *treeness?* What makes an apple tree different than an oak tree? Since they are both trees, in what ways are they both the same? If an apple tree didn't produce apples, it would not fulfill part of its final cause. We could say that it doesn't deliver the *good* for which it was created. We might cut it down and cast it into the fire.

All created things fall short in some way from fulfilling their formal cause and their final cause. Every home ever built has some minor imperfections; aspects that don't exactly meet the blueprint. Every home will have some limitations and compromises in how it meets its multiple purposes of shelter, climate control, efficiency, and comfort.

In the same way, every human being, to different degrees, falls short of his formal cause, of what it means to be a perfect human being. We all have some slight physical or mental defects, ways in which we deviate from our formal cause or blueprint, but we are still called to try to meet some basic purposes, the goods associated with being human.

I have previously referred to Lewis's book, *The Abolition of Man*, and how he discussed a universal set of moral laws which he called the *Tao*. In effect, the *Tao* is what we call the natural law. Natural law essentially derives from a combination of our formal cause and our final cause as human beings. It is the moral law which is derived from our understanding of human nature; what human beings are meant to do and how they are intended to behave based on their causes. Because human beings also have freedom, they do not always act in the way their creator intended for them. In the following passage, Lewis uses one of his own character traits as an example of how it deviates from what a human being should do. He recognizes it as an imperfection to his humanness.

> Those who know the *Tao* can hold that to call children delightful or old men venerable is not simply to record a psychological fact about our own parental or filial emotions at the moment, but to recognize a quality which *demands* a certain response from us whether we make it or not. I myself do not enjoy the society of small children: because I speak from within the *Tao* I recognize

this as a defect in myself—just as a man may have to recognize that he is tone deaf or color blind.

C.S. Lewis, *The Abolition of Man*

Sometimes when, in our weakness, we fail to meet some expected standard of behavior, we use the excuse that we are *only* human. But this is not a proper assessment. We fail because we are *imperfectly* human. It is the flaws in our construction, a product of both nature and nurture and of the concupiscence associated with original sin, which hinder our ability to be fully human and to do what we ought to do at all times. And we pray in confidence that a merciful God will take our imperfections into account when our behavior is judged on the last day; that our inclination to do things that we want, but which are against our human nature, will somehow mitigate the judgment we deserve.

At the same time, however, we cannot sit back complacently and contently in our state of imperfection. We are called to try to grow in virtue, to overcome our flaws and not use them as excuses, and certainly not to use them as a reason for pride or celebration. Our final cause is to be fully human; this is what will ultimately bring us true happiness.

Sometimes we use objects or things for other than their intended purposes. We essentially give an object a different final cause than was intended when it was created. Let's look at a book as an example. In general, its formal cause is a combination of all those things that make a book a book. We might refer to a dictionary to determine the definition of a book. Adding to the formal cause are those specific words and concepts that make a particular book unique. The material cause for a book is the combination of paper and ink used in its construction. Its efficient cause can be seen from different perspectives as the author or the publisher. But what is the final cause of a book, its purpose for being created? Well, that will be different for each particular book. For example, the purpose of this book is to instruct and inspire you by sharing insights which will help you make good decisions on your life journey.

Suppose I read an inspiring book and believe that one of my parishioners may find it beneficial. And so I give that person a copy of the book as a gift. What do you think would be my reaction if I visited her home and found that instead of reading the book that she was using it to prop open a door? Obviously, the book could function as a doorstop, but that was not its intended purpose, its final cause.

We can often go astray on our journey when we lose sight of the final causes of things around us. We sometimes use things for good purposes, disregarding that we may not be using them for their ultimate purpose. And, unfortunately, we sometimes use things for purposes that contradict their ultimate purpose.

We can look at the growing problem of eating disorders. The purpose of food is to provide us with nutrition to sustain life, but God also created us with taste buds so that we can enjoy our food and find eating to be pleasurable. When we get confused and associate the pleasure of eating as its purpose, rather than as an enjoyable side effect, then problems can result. It can lead to obesity. Or it can lead to purging to allow the pleasure of eating while completely denying its purpose, its final cause of nutrition.

And, in an analogous way, we can consider the serious abuses of human sexuality. The final cause of sexuality is procreation. God created the sexual organs of men and women to be different, but complementary, so that they could unite and create new life to sustain and expand the human population. The formal causes of men and women are slightly different so that they can become one and fulfill a combined final cause. And yes, God made sexual intercourse pleasurable, but this is not its purpose; it is rather a wonderful side effect. When contraception became widely accepted in our culture, it was in effect a societal statement that the purpose of human sexuality had changed; the final cause was now considered to be pleasure. Society decided that we could enjoy the pleasure of sex whenever we wished and determined that conceiving a child was simply a side effect which we could learn how to avoid. It's similar to purging.

Pope Paul VI, in his encyclical "Humanae Vitae" issued in 1968, points out the problem of this approach. He indirectly refers to the formal cause, efficient cause, and final cause of our sexuality when he states:

> They must also recognize that an act of mutual love which impairs the capacity to transmit life which God the Creator, through specific laws, has built into it, frustrates His design which constitutes the norm of marriage, and contradicts the will of the Author of life. Hence to use this divine gift while depriving it, even if only partially, of its meaning and purpose, is equally repugnant to the nature of man and of woman, and is consequently in opposition to the plan of God and His holy will.
>
> Pope Paul VI, "Humanae Vitae"

And this acceptance of a new understanding of sexuality by society opened the door for a host of abuses as predicted by the pope. He predicted that contraception would lead to increased infidelity and spousal abuse, government-mandated contraception to restrict family size, and a general decay in moral standards. It also led to the Roe v. Wade decision only five years later that legalized abortion, the ultimate form of purging.

It is a continual struggle to identify our own purpose in life, our own individual final cause. We often make many good choices, but is there one best choice that we often fail to identify or pursue? There is a balance we must achieve between making rash judgments and the inability to make decisions at all. It is good to stop now and then and make sure we know who we are and where we are on our life journey.

We may stay in a dead-end job, for example, because it provides us with many good things. It might give us financial security that allows us to support our family, and that is a very good thing and can be a very big factor in our happiness. We are sometimes called to make sacrifices out of love for our families, from a Christian perspective, to pick up our crosses. But sometimes we need to reassess and be honest about our reasons for not making changes. Is love of family the real reason for staying in a miserable job, or is it fear, insecurity, laziness, or a lack of faith and trust that prevents us from pursuing our true vocation?

Convincing us that we are doing good things is often a tool of the devil. He can convince us to do good things to prevent us from doing great things. The Boy Scout can become so busy doing the good deed of helping little old ladies cross the street that he ignores his calling to be a great traffic engineer and developing methods to improve the safety for all who need to get to the other side of the road. Helping one person along their journey is a good thing. Using our talents to help many people on their journeys is a great thing. So we sometimes need to stop and reflect on our calling. Sometimes we need to be willing to take one step backward to get around an obstacle before we can jump five steps forward. But it can be a scary maneuver.

As human beings, we all have a generic final cause in common. But our individual callings or vocations give each of us unique component of that final cause. Do you know yours? When was the last time you thought about it?

There is a wonderful story in Christian scriptures which is usually referred to as the story of the rich, young man. It goes like this:

> Now someone approached him and said, "Teacher, what good must I do to gain eternal life?" He answered him, "Why do you ask me about the good? There is only One who is good. If you wish to enter into life, keep the commandments." He asked him, "Which ones?" And Jesus replied, "'You shall not kill; you shall not commit adultery; you shall not steal; you shall not bear false witness; honor your father and your mother'; and 'you shall love your neighbor as yourself.'" The young man said to him, "All of these I have observed. What do I still lack?" Jesus said to him, "If you wish to be perfect, go, sell what you have and give to (the) poor, and you will have treasure in heaven. Then come, follow me." When the young man heard this statement, he went away sad, for he had many possessions.
>
> Matthew 19:16–22

The young man was a good man living a good life. But Jesus gave him direction for his life's journey that would make him great. We may not all be called to sell everything, but we need to think about what we ought to do and not just what we want to do.

REASONED SPEECH VERSUS RHETORIC

> Nature, as we say, does nothing without some purpose; and for the purpose of making man a politi-

cal animal she has endowed him alone among the animals with the power of reasoned speech.

Aristotle

Rational beings will try to determine what is good, what is true, what is right, so that they can make choices that will lead to happiness. It's part of our final cause. One can imagine Socrates and the Greek philosophers debating and questioning one another to determine the right way that man should behave in the world; what a good man should do to create a good society and please the gods, in effect, trying to determine how does man fulfill the natural law. And what one imagines is very different from what one observes when they view their representatives and senators debating and questioning issues of our time in Washington.

In philosophy class, we learned about the difference between the reasoned speech of philosophers and the rhetoric of the poets. Philosophy proves; poetry persuades. The poets express opinions, positions that are not justified by facts and reasons. Sometimes these opinions are true, and sometimes they are false. But even when they are true, the poet does not attempt to show why they must be true as the philosopher does. The poet uses his gifts of persuasion rather than logical arguments to try to convince others of the validity of his position.

Our politicians, and to a certain degree our news media representatives, are the poets of today. We watch a debate during the election season and are immediately inundated with a variety of opinions trying to spin the results. It is no longer a deep search for truths to apply to today's world, to determine what is the good thing to do as a society. It is a superficial debate with rhetoric not philosophical discussion. It is not about determining the truth. The goal of the politician is to give his constituents what they want, not what is necessarily good for them.

And sometimes what the constituents want is to simply hear reassuring words that may be void of any content. During the 2008 presidential campaign, a prominent radio talk show host would often comment about one of the candidates that, "He can say nothing better than anyone else." It was a backhanded compliment in a way, but I think it was more of a criticism aimed at the American public who rallied around hollow speeches, who were more interested in feeling good than honestly attacking the realities of our problems. We have lost a desire to pursue the truth and to be fully human.

Doing philosophy can fall into two categories; it can be contemplative or contentious. Contemplative philosophy consists of thinking and pursuing truth for the enjoyment of understanding the world around us. It creates, for me, an image of college professors sitting around smoking pipes, thinking deep thoughts. Contentious philosophy, however, is philosophy directed to arguing against opinions, especially false opinions. But we don't seem to want to hear about contention anymore. There are too many of the sentiment that says: *Why can't we all just get along?* It has become politically correct to abandon the search for the truth in exchange for a sense of peace. But it is a false sense of peace. It is bad poetry. Only the truth can lead us to true happiness.

And the worst poetry of our day is moral relativism; the belief that there is no absolute truth. Of course, this opinion can clearly be seen to be self-contradictory. If there is no absolute truth, then the statement, *there is no absolute truth,* cannot be absolutely true. If you read the statement, *do not believe anything you read,* there is no reason to believe it.

When you have been waiting in line for forty-five minutes at the amusement park to ride the roller coaster, and someone cuts into the line and steps in front of you, you immediately know that this is unfair. It is an absolute. You don't rationalize that even though you consider this behavior to be wrong, that it may not be wrong in the other person's value set, and therefore it is acceptable. No, you want justice.

But despite its obvious logical flaws, the bad poetry of moral relativism is not challenged except by moral leaders. The moral leaders are like voices crying out in the wilderness trying to instruct people that there is a straight path. But moral relativism promises pleasure, and most do not want to entertain any argument that would interfere with that pursuit. We are prone to readily exchange happiness in eternity for short-term pleasure today. In choosing the smooth path through life, we do not want to consider that it might not lead us safely to our desired ultimate Point B.

SUMMARY

In looking for the correct path through life, it is important to use your God-given gift of rationality. As one of my high school teachers used to put it, "Use your head for something other than a hat rack." Hopefully the reflections offered in this chapter can help you consider how to be a more reasoning person; to *do* philosophy for yourself.

Use distinctions to frame discussions; it will save you a lot of frustration. But remember that it takes a great deal of discipline, especially upfront, to agree on definitions. It would make no sense to sit on a jury in a capital murder case without first understanding the definition of capital murder.

Consider how categories and causes can be applied to issues and controversies of today to provide a structured approach to problem solving in society and in your own home. Just because you may have natural desires which lead you to behaviors that contradict natural law does not justify your submission to those desires. You need to strive to be *completely* human, not just *only* human. Work to understand your own individual calling. You may not reach your target, but it is important to keep trying. As Mother Teresa said, "God hasn't called me to be successful. He's called me to be faithful."

Try to focus on the truth and not be led astray down wrong paths by skillful and melodic poetry. Take responsibility for holding politicians accountable for what they say, and do not accept their words simply because they make you feel good at the moment. Our actions, or inactions, today will have consequences tomorrow. Search for truth that will lead you to happiness, not poetry that will result only in fleeting emotions.

LABELS
(Whose Team Are You On?)

I was born and raised a Catholic and have attended church regularly every Sunday all of my life. For most of that time, I prayed and worshipped without much concern for the politics and preferences of the pastor or the community around me. Sure, I knew that there were some priests that seemed to express views that were more consistent with my own, that spoke on subjects that were of greater interest to me. And the music at different Masses had different levels of compatibility with my tastes. But, all in all, I attended the parish that was the closest to where I lived. Even if I had differences with the pastor, it was my church and my community, and I was staying at my local parish out of a combination of convenience and loyalty. Church politics was not one of those areas that were important for me.

In 1993, however, our family experienced a significant time of spiritual conversion and our lives changed considerably. My wife and I made changes to our lifestyle as we were drawn to a closer relationship with God. We prayed more often, and we prayed together. We were led to a more active participation in the Catholic Church and its activities. I came to realize how little I knew about my faith, even though I had been a practicing Catholic all my life and had attended Catholic grade school for eight years. And so we tried to learn by reading books and listening to tapes. I met more people, listened and paid attention a little more closely to what was going on around me, and studied so that I could learn more about the Catholic Church and her teachings. And as I did these things, I was awakened to the riches and treasures of the Church, but I also uncovered a great number of divisions within our Catholic community that I had been oblivious to in the past.

In 1995, I began taking classes at Sacred Heart Major Seminary in Detroit, and from 1996 through 1999 was in formation to become a permanent deacon. During those years, the polarization caused by some of these underlying divisions became even more evident to me. There were us-versus-them conflicts around every corner, and my goal, as I was ordained in 1999, was to be a bridge builder. It's a goal that I still hang on to, but I fail more often than I succeed.

BUILDING BRIDGES

In an us-versus-them world, the first order of business is to pick up sides. Who's on our team and who's not? And this requires putting people into one of two major categories. In today's society, we often find it convenient to use the labels *conservative* and *liberal* as the broadest level of filter. These labels exist in our society, and they also exist in the Church. But in the Church, actually only a small portion of the members participate in the us-versus-them battles. Those that do, however, comprise very committed factions. Still, most Catholic parishioners go about their Sunday worship much like I did for many years, unaware that there is even a battle taking place.

As I was in formation for the diaconate, for receiving the sacrament of holy orders, I was exposed to faculty members, classmates, seminarians, and clergy with different spiritualities, world views, and experiences. I attended a broader range of churches in the Archdiocese of Detroit and experienced a greater level of diversity in the celebration of the liturgy, the prayer of the people, the focus of the pastor, and the involvement of the laity. So when I met with people on my team (I was generally considered to be on the conservative team, albeit a weak member), I would be queried for my opinions on whether Bishop So-and-so, whether Father So-and-so, or whether St. So-and-so Parish was conservative or liberal.

It was an issue that surfaced more obviously as I began to choose where I would serve my first diaconal assignment after ordination. If there was any ambiguity during the previous years, it was now time to declare which team I chose to be on. It was at this time that I realized how poorly the conservative/liberal labeling system fit for dealing with Catholic Church issues and how I didn't want to be assigned either label in this context. The divide was a deep chasm that neither side really wanted to be bridged. The one side was associated with the Call to Holiness conference; the other side had the Call to Action conference. Both sides had Catholic magazines and newspapers that championed their causes and opinions. Each side had key bishops that were their leaders and representatives.

While I shared more in common, and felt more comfortable, with people who considered themselves conservatives, I didn't like the label for myself. This was, in part, because acquiring any label makes it difficult to build bridges. But, more importantly, I came to the understanding that the conservative/liberal labeling system is not an appropriate one for the matters being debated and argued in the Church. There were serious divisions between the two factions, but what was their source? Could the chasm be bridged?

To build bridges, there needs to be some common ground and room for discussion between groups on either end of the span. The factions may disagree on an issue or have different priorities, but there cannot be complete disdain for those on the opposite bank. And it seems that it should be possible to have discussions and cooperation between people with conservative and liberal approaches to solving problems. But it became clear that the differences between the two groups of Catholics hiding under conservative/liberal labels involved something much deeper. There was a desire by those immersed in battle to make the chasm greater, not to build bridges. Some differences between groups could be tolerated, but apparently others could not.

ACCEPTABLE DIFFERENCES

I shopped to find my first parish, a community where I would feel comfortable, and with a pastor who had a spirituality that would be compatible with mine—compatible, not the same. There are parishes with old, ornate buildings and others with modern auditorium-style facilities. There are some that are large with professional music ministries with elaborate, well-rehearsed choirs and some that are small with volunteer musicians and ad hoc choirs. Some sing traditional songs in Latin accompanied by an organ, others sing contemporary songs accompanied by guitars and drums. Some focus on traditional devotions, such as the rosary and Eucharistic adoration, some focus on charismatic devotions and pray in tongues, and some focus on scripture studies. And all of these differences are acceptable differences, and most of them can be described using labels such as traditional, contemporary, maybe even progressive. But none can be truly classified as conservative or liberal. None of these differences cause irreconcilable polarities and, in fact, many coexist peacefully within any given parish. Sometimes the traditional group and the contemporary group don't understand each other. This can result in some animosities over usually trivial issues, and this is where a bridge builder can be effective.

Personally, I am more comfortable with the traditional perspective. I prefer adoration, praying the rosary and the Stations of the Cross, and reading scripture than speaking in tongues and being slain in the Spirit. I prefer an old-fashioned church building to a modern one. I enjoy organ and piano music to guitars and drums. But I realized that none of the differences listed above were major differences that would prevent me from serving and ministering at a parish. All of these differences are acceptable differences, and I could imagine myself effectively bridging between various groups to bring a community together more closely.

CONSERVATIVE VERSUS LIBERAL

The conservative and liberal labels do have meaning, but they are overused and misused and unnecessarily set well-meaning folks against each other. They deal more correctly with differences in methods of problem resolution, the means, than they do with the goal being addressed, the end. Being conservative or liberal is a difference, not a distinction. I do not believe you can answer the question: *Are you conservative or not conservative?* There is no concrete definition for a conservative or a liberal; it is a continuum and can vary depending on the scope of the issue. One may be morally liberal, socially moderate, and fiscally conservative.

Back in 2000, I traveled with six other deacons on a short pilgrimage to Haiti with the relief organization Food for the Poor. We encountered the poorest of the poor. We saw the hope in Food for the Poor sponsored orphanages, schools, vocation centers, feeding centers, hospitals, and other humanitarian projects. We also saw the despair in the faces of the multitude living in the slums with deplorable living conditions. We looked into the faces of parents who could not give their children any hope for a brighter future.

And as we sat back reflecting on our experiences after a day touring the slums, one of my fellow deacons lamented about his frustration in his ministry back at home. It seems he could not get other deacons to participate in his protests, picketing, and boycotts aimed at preventing companies from using sweatshop laborers to produce their goods. His contention was that those who did not participate in his protests did not care about the poor. Of course, this contention is false. We can agree that we should help the poor but disagree on where to put our efforts and the best way to accomplish this goal.

Helping the people of Haiti is very complex. On one level, we can give them food, we can build homes for them, and we can dig wells to provide them with clean drinking water. On another level, we can provide them with job training, with vocational equipment such as sewing machines and mechanics tools, and with farm equipment to grow crops and raise livestock. We can attack the problems from a political perspective and work to build a government that is free of corruption so that the country can once again be self-sufficient, so that people can raise their families in safety and security.

There are many ways to help the poor, and we all have differing opinions on which way is the best, and this is where conservative and liberal labels are often appropriate. Personally, I consider myself a social conservative. I prefer teaching someone to fish rather than giving him a fish; but I do recognize the need to give that person food until he is able to provide for himself.

In our country, almost all people share the same desires for peace, for national security, for good health care and education, for retirement security, and for the elimination of poverty. But we disagree greatly on the best means to reach these good ends. And these disagreements can lead to significant divisions and animosity between the camps that argue for liberal approaches and those that argue for conservative approaches. But as strong as the debate is on these social issues, I do not see any of these as insurmountable, as chasms that cannot be bridged.

UNACCEPTABLE DIFFERENCES

What makes some differences so great that the divide between opposing groups cannot be spanned? What accounts for these serious, unacceptable differences that cannot be tolerated? The answer is that one of the sides of the debate sees the issue as a black-and-white issue, as a matter of right and wrong. It is no longer a matter of preferring one particular means to the same common end. It is recognizing that your opponent has chosen an approach that you not only don't prefer but that you cannot accept in good conscience. It is sometimes disagreeing not only with your opponent's means but also his end.

A more fitting label pair to use in these cases is orthodox versus unorthodox; they create a distinction. You may remember from the introduction that the word *orthodox* means straight or correct belief. We all have beliefs about actions and behaviors that we consider non-negotiable; some have a great number and others have very few. But in situations where these moral beliefs are involved, we can accept that there is only one correct path. We cannot, in good conscience, allow ourselves to compromise the *Tao*. In these situations, we are faced with a distinction: *Is the action or decision orthodox or not orthodox?* In other words, we look to see if choosing one side of an issue is in conflict with our moral compass.

What is interesting in these conflicts is that those on the opposite side of the issue often don't feel as strongly; they see it as a matter of strong preference rather than a necessity. One side sees no room for compromise, but the other might consider compromise if approached in the proper manner.

These unacceptable differences are what I found at the heart of many of the divisions in the Catholic Church. They were matters of orthodoxy, not conservatism. And these matters of orthodoxy fell generally into three categories: moral, doctrinal, and liturgical. While the issues in all three categories were seen as equally black-and-white, the impact of abuses in these categories was not seen as equally severe. Liturgical abuses, for example, are not seen to be as scandalous as abuses of moral teachings, but they are seen as an indicator of disobedience. They are a sign that other abuses are right around the corner or festering under the surface, what some refer to as being on a slippery slope.

The Church publishes a document called the *General Instruction on the Roman Missal* (GIRM) which outlines all the instructions for the proper liturgical celebration of the Mass. It directs, for example, when the people should sit, stand, and kneel. It instructs the priest regarding proper postures such as when to bow or genuflect. The GIRM is an official Church document with only a few opportunities for local bishops to make adjustments to meet their specific situations. Priests and their congregations are expected to be obedient to the instructions given in the GIRM as interpreted by their bishop. Unfortunately, very few parishes completely follow all the prescriptions set down in this document. Church members who know about the GIRM and want to be obedient become very upset when the priest or worship commission takes liberties with the approved procedures simply because of their personal preferences.

Most people in the pews, however, don't know what the GIRM says or that it even exists. They simply follow the direction of the priest or those liturgists that he appoints and tacitly approves. Most parishioners follow like good sheep. The good news for them is that they are being obedient to the priest and, since they do not know that what they are doing is against the rules, they do not become preoccupied and distracted. This allows them to participate more fully in the liturgy. Those that know about the GIRM, however, know that being obedient to the priest means being disobedient to the bishop and the

Church. And this tears them apart. The result is a Mass where some people stand or sit during the consecration at the direction of the priest, while others kneel according to the instructions in the GIRM. Instead of the unity of celebration intended by the GIRM, confusion and distractions are created. Most of the people who are standing would gladly kneel if they knew that it was the correct posture, if only the priest would give them sound instruction.

Some try to add to the confusion by setting up false polarities, much as my deacon friend did in Haiti. They criticize those concerned about proper liturgical postures, for example, and comment that they should be more concerned about helping the poor instead of worrying about when to kneel. The implication becomes that those who want to kneel at the proper times do not care about the poor. It's not very good logic, of course. It's not an either/or situation, it's a both/and. There are two different distinctions, although not of equal importance: *Should you follow the GIRM or not?* and *Should you help the poor or not?*

The GIRM is a changeable document; the Church adapts it over time. It is not like matters of morals and doctrine which are unchangeable. The GIRM is man-made law, but the Church establishes who has the authority to change it. Violating these laws is not as serious as violating God's laws, and many of the differences between unorthodox priests and orthodox faithful can still be bridged. As a deacon, I prefer to be assigned to a parish where the pastor follows the letter of the GIRM, but I am able to tolerate some minor deviations and am willing to consider special needs for exceptions, such as limitations of a church facility.

At the other end of the spectrum from liturgical abuses is the area of abuses of moral and doctrinal teachings. Catholics are expected to accept the teaching authority of the Church, what we call the Magesterium. There is a set of non-negotiable teachings that, in effect, define what it means to be Catholic. And, based on these teachings, one can effectively set up the distinction: *Are you Catholic or not Catholic?* I am afraid that there would be a wide disparity if we compared the number of people who would fit this definition for being Catholic and the number of people who claim to be Catholic.

The Catholic Church is particularly clear about her moral teachings regarding issues such as abortion, contraception, sex outside of marriage, homosexuality, and embryonic stem cell research. Therefore, a Catholic, some might say a faithful Catholic, accepts the Church's position on these issues as orthodox teachings which cannot be compromised. Problems arise when members of the clergy or groups within the Church publicly take positions that are contrary to orthodox Church teaching. These situations result in unacceptable differences that cannot be tolerated by the orthodox faithful.

A pastor who supports contraception and tells his parishioners that it is their own personal decision whether to incorporate it into their marriages is clearly spreading unorthodox teaching and leading his congregation away from the truth. Groups, such as Catholics for Free Choice, that openly support the acceptability of a pro-choice position on abortion are more than liberal; they are unorthodox and not truly Catholic organizations. Those that promote the ordination of women to the priesthood, even though the Church has ruled infallibly against this possibility, pursue an unorthodox position. Parishes that hold liturgies to celebrate gay lifestyles are distorting what the Church teaches and confusing both their own congregations as well as the community at large. These are serious issues and differences that cannot be bridged. Those that hold to orthodox Catholic teachings on these matters see no common ground; there is no opportunity for compromise. They have no desire to consider building bridges to the other side.

APPLICATIONS ON OUR JOURNEY

I have spent most of this chapter so far discussing issues very specific to my Catholic faith and ministry. But I believe that the issues and topics presented within that environment are very generic and translate to many of the situations we encounter on our journeys. We are exposed to the overuse and misuse of labels. We see divisive efforts to polarize people into competing groups when they could actually be comfortable in both groups. We are faced with battles in which we find no room for compromise. And we all use labels ourselves.

When we meet or encounter people for the first time, there is a natural tendency for us to try to categorize them, to put labels on them. It's not usually a conscious effort, but we look for ways in which that person is like us and ways in which that person is different from us, especially in areas that are very important to us. For the political activist, it may be determining whether the new acquaintance is a Democrat or a Republican. For the stock market enthusiast, it may be whether he is a bear or a bull. For others, it may be simply whether the other person is right-brained or left-brained. Are they richer or poorer than us? What is the person's race, ethnicity, gender, sexual orientation, age, and moral viewpoint?

Understanding the background and preferences of the people we meet can be very useful as we try to relate to them and understand their behavior. It can help avoid conflicts and provide knowledge on how to work and live together. These labels, however, can also become obstacles to clear vision as we try to solve problems in our lives and in our society. Lines of demarcation can be drawn that separate people into competing groups, and every battle becomes framed as an us-versus-them conflict. We can relinquish our individual vision for the future and adopt the broader vision of the team. Or, worse yet, we can fail to form our own vision at all and instead look to our team to tell us what it should be.

What teams do you belong to? Maybe it's your political party, your church affiliation, your labor union, or a professional association. Maybe it's a special interest group representing a portion of the population, such as women, blacks, Hispanics, homosexuals, or retirees.

When I was in my early fifties, I didn't feel old; I was still gainfully employed. But suddenly, I was bombarded with requests in the mail to join AARP, formerly the American Association of Retired Persons. They promoted a host of benefits and discounts I could enjoy by becoming a member. But, even though some of these benefits are attractive, I have resisted joining because I disagree with many of the organization's political views and positions. In joining, I would effectively sell my vote. I would save money on hotel rooms and insurance, but they would use my dues to influence legislation contrary to my beliefs. The AARP wants to present itself as representing all Americans older than fifty, which is about thirty percent of our U.S. population and about forty percent of those old enough to vote, according to the Census Bureau's estimates for 2007. I am annoyed when I see politicians listening to the AARP as if they speak as one voice for over ninety million citizens. Us old folks represent a very diverse group indeed; we do not think as a bloc and should not vote as one.

How do your teams influence how you think and how you act? Are you able to keep your independence, or do you compromise your beliefs for the good of the team? Do you search independently for the truth, or do you depend on your team to make judgments for you? Do you hold your teams accountable so that they do not use your resources against your interests?

Many times the teams we choose to join, or are required to join, overstep their bounds. We must maintain a level of independence and not let special interest groups tell us what to believe and how to vote. We must be willing to put in the effort to be philosophers and search out the truth. We must search out what we ought to do and believe, not what others want us to do and believe.

And at this point you may argue that I am contradicting myself, that I support letting one of my teams, the Catholic Church, define my vision on many key issues, but then caution against letting your team tell you what to do. In response, let's go back and look again at what we know by faith and by reason.

FAITH AND REASON REVISITED

If we have a trustworthy source of information, we can start by believing that information with faith and then worry about understanding it later. For me, the Catholic Church is the ultimate source for interpreting God's revelation to man and guiding me to what I ought to do. To justify my trust in the Church, I can revisit the three questions proposed in the "Faith and Reason" chapter to determine the basis for my faith in the Catholic Church to provide me with direction in my life. Those three questions dealt with the issues of honesty, freedom from conflict of interest, and competence.

Do I think that Church leadership has been honest and trustworthy? Yes, I do. To be sure, there have been individuals who have failed in upholding their responsibilities and who have not been worthy of the trust bestowed upon them, but these are relatively few. I prefer to look to Jesus Christ, the cornerstone, and to the many saints, especially the martyrs, who are living stones that have built a new spiritual house. Many of our popes were among those martyrs and gave up their lives rather than compromise the truth. I look at all the priests and religious who have given up and committed their entire lives, sacrificing families and careers, to be at the service of others. There have been many sacrifices in pursuit of the truth. Some may fail to live up to Church teachings; they have weaknesses, they are sinners like all of us. But the teachings don't change just because they are difficult to follow.

Is the Church non-biased or does she have something to gain by me choosing to accept her teachings? It may seem ironic, but the most comforting aspect of my Catholic faith is that the Church is not a democracy. The Church presents what she believes to be the teachings of Jesus, even when she knows that these teachings will not be popular with her members and may cause many to leave. We don't get to vote on what is right and wrong, and that is good because if we did we would succumb to the tendency to rationalization, to interpret God's revelation to match our will, not God's will. For example, the Church teaches her members that contraception is wrong because she cares for our souls, not because she will gain if we accept that teaching. She may be actually hurt financially when people walk away.

Is the Church knowledgeable on the subject matter? The Church has been in existence for 2,000 years. Inspired by the Holy Spirit, she defined the canon of writings that constitute the book we now call the Bible and provided that book as a gift to the world. The foundations of the Church's interpretations of those writings date back to the first centuries, to those we call the Church fathers who were familiar with the nuances of the languages and customs of the time when they were written. The Church is the home of great philosophers, such as Augustine and Thomas Aquinas, who have worked to show how our faith is reasonable. Faced with the effort and commitment that has been expended over 2,000 years of Catholic Church history, I am humbled. I can identify no other organization that has a comparable level of knowledge for me to turn to for direction on matters of faith and morals.

And so I can personally look at these three questions and conclude that, on matters within her jurisdiction, I should start by believing Church teaching. If I am faced with situations on my life journey that conflict with what she teaches, then the burden is on me to turn to reason and understand the conflict, to determine reasons why I might be right and the Church wrong. I cannot simply have an *opinion* that the Church is wrong and to say it is a matter of my conscience. I have to form that conscience philosophically. I have an obligation to study the Church's foundation for her teaching and determine where she is in error; otherwise it is purely rationalization on my part. If I ignore Church teaching without justification, I am merely deciding to do what I want rather than what I ought.

This same analysis can be considered for other sources of information in life that we trust. But most of our sources of information, most of the teams we belong to, don't meet the three requirements for deserving our faith with the same level of confidence. How do your teams stack up? Are they honest, free from bias, and competent? Are their recommendations worthy of your trust? These are good questions to ask along our journey.

During my career at General Motors, there were many occasions when we, the employees, were encouraged to express the team's position on various legislation to our members of congress. Once, for example, we were encouraged to support action granting preferred trading status for China. Before I could do this, however, I first needed to evaluate the request against my three criteria to determine if I could honor it in good faith. I could look at the third criterion and believe that the GM management team was knowledgeable on the matter; we had plants in China and management knew about market demographics for automobiles in the region. But, without even considering the honesty issue, I was reluctant to put my faith in them on this matter, because there was a business advantage for GM to opening up trade in China. My second criterion was in question. GM had something to gain by my action of contacting my senator and representative. This didn't mean that supporting the legislation was wrong; it just meant I couldn't support it on faith alone just because I was a member of the team. And so I looked for another source of information that I believed to be honest, and that was the United States Conference of Catholic Bishops (USCCB). On their Web site I found a position paper that argued against the legislation on the grounds that it implicitly condoned China's abuses of human rights. I sent a copy of that position paper, along with my own thoughts, up through the GM management chain, and it eventually arrived on the desk of a corporate lawyer who had been stationed in China for several years. I was surprised when I received a thoughtful reply from him which detailed his experience-based opinion that opening up China to free trade would be a positive step for human rights because it would open up their society and expose abuses that had been kept hidden from the world. And so, I had to consider that maybe he had a more knowledgeable perspective than the U.S. bishops on this matter.

On another occasion, we were encouraged to financially support the GM political action committee (PAC). And so I first investigated which politicians the committee had supported in the past. And I compared that list to a list of politicians that supported partial-birth abortion; an important *unacceptable difference* for me. And when I did, I found a very high correlation between these two groups. Obviously, the GM PAC did not support the candidates because of their abortion stance; that was not a matter of interest to them as it was to me. They funded these politicians because they supported nationalized health care that would be very advantageous to GM because it would shift health care costs from corporations to the government. It just so happened that those on the team that support liberal social programs such as national health care also follow their team's radical pro-choice positions as well. I concluded that I could not support the recommendation of my GM management team because my contributions to the PAC would indirectly benefit candidates that I opposed on moral grounds.

Corporations have their interests and so do other organizations such as labor unions. After my retirement from General Motors, I decided to go back to school to pursue a teacher certification program with the intention of possibly becoming a high school physics and mathematics teacher as a second career. In one of the introductory classes, the instructor invited the president of a local teachers' union to address the class and share his perspectives. In preparation for our speaker, our instructor asked the class, "What do teachers' unions do?" I immediately raised my hand and responded, "They support pro-choice politicians." I could tell from the expression on her face that this was not the answer she was looking for.

When our speaker arrived, I questioned him about why the National Education Association (NEA), to which his organization was affiliated, had to take such extremely liberal stances on issues such as abortion, same-sex marriage, and distribution of contraceptives which had nothing to do with teaching, negotiating contracts, and protecting teachers' rights. He responded by trying to give justifications on how each of these issues was important to providing a classroom environment conducive to learning. But the arguments were shallow. They were rationalizations. The political team that happens to support all of these liberal moral issues also happens to be the team that supports greater funding for education, smaller class sizes, and stronger union protection. When you sign up with the team that will help you be a better teacher and helps you better earn a living for your family, you have to be a good team player and support their other issues as well. There is a certain level of *quid pro quo* that exists.

A large portion of a teacher's union dues goes to support liberal causes in exchange for improved pay, job security, and work conditions; even if those causes conflict with the individual teacher's moral beliefs. In 2008, the California Teachers Association spent over one million dollars of its members' dues to try to defeat Proposal 8, which would define marriage as between one man and one woman. They also opposed Proposal 4, which would require parental notification for abortions. Is this the purpose of labor unions? Is this the appropriate way to spend union dues when many of the California teachers supported both of these proposals based on strong moral beliefs?

A CNN report on exit polls taken during the 2004 election indicated that approximately forty percent of union voters cast their ballot for George Bush. But while two out of five union members voted for the Republican candidate for president, essentially all of union financial support went to support Democratic candidates. Are dues from Republican union members being used to help defeat candidates they support?

As a non-union worker at General Motors, I could review the issues and candidates supported by the GM PAC and decide whether I wanted to participate or not. If I were to become a teacher, however, it would be more difficult to avoid contributing money to the union that would be spent to support causes I found morally reprehensible. Unions effectively act as PACs, with 30–70 percent of funds collected from dues allocated to advancing political issues and candidates.

There are some *right to work* states that allow workers to decide whether they join a union or not. And in various states there is different legislation, such as *paycheck protection* laws designed to protect workers from contributing to political causes involuntarily. There are also options available to register as a *religious objector* or as an *agency fee payer*. Many teachers and other union members who do not agree with their union's political agenda pursue none of these options, however, because of the complexity of the paperwork and procedures and because of fear of retaliation for not supporting the team.

PARTISAN POLITICS

One of the greatest obstacles preventing our society from growing out of its adolescence is the polarization caused by our two-party political system. What has been a good system in the past has deteriorated to something that resembles a teenage gang war. There is a fight over blue turf and red turf. It's a struggle for power, and no tactics are considered inappropriate. Politicians support team members even when they are wrong and criticize those on the opponents team even when they do something right.

While I believe that the divisiveness is stronger now than in recent past, I was curious to read an account in scripture that indicated some of the same behaviors existed 2,000 years ago. At that time, it wasn't Democrats and Republicans; it was Pharisees and Sadducees. The evangelist Luke tells this story in the Acts of the Apostles:

> When Paul noticed that some were Sadducees and others were Pharisees, he called out in the council, "Brothers, I am a Pharisee, a son of Pharisees. I am on trial concerning the hope of the resurrection of the dead." When he said this, a dissension began between the Pharisees and the Sadducees, and the assembly was divided. (The Sadducees say that there is no resurrection, or angel, or spirit; but the Pharisees acknowledge all three.) Then a great clamor arose, and certain scribes of the Pharisees' group stood up and contended, "We find nothing wrong with this man. What if a spirit or an angel has spoken to him?" When the dissension became violent, the tribune, fearing

that they would tear Paul to pieces, ordered the soldiers to go down, take him by force, and bring him into the barracks.

Acts 23:6–10

The Pharisees supported Paul just because he was a Pharisee, and tempers and emotions flared. Our current dissention is nothing new, but it is nonetheless troublesome. The Democratic and Republican Parties represent teams locked in an us-versus-them battle that often appears to disregard the best interest of the country. Winning the major battles, even if it means compromising national interests, is important for establishing a strong base of power. This drive for power results in irrationally attacking and finding fault in everything the leaders of the other team try to do or say. And this interferes with any progress toward compromise. When you work hard to portray the opponents as a bunch of incompetents, you cannot dare admit that they may have an intelligent proposal; it would undermine all your efforts.

And the parties vote on most legislation and on most appointments as blocs, according to their party platform. A politician who is pro-life and pro-union, for example, would find it difficult to find a home in either party and would never make it to any major office, even though his views might be more representative of the population of his state than those of either major party. When we vote, we don't select those who have views most similar to our own, we vote for the best of two compromises. A small handful of party activists set up two polarizing agendas, and our only choice is to pick one of them; we can't pick something in the middle.

If political party power is split in Washington between the executive and legislative branches, it is difficult to get anything accomplished. The parties rally their team members to vote as blocs. Individual members of congress compromise their own beliefs out of fear of chastisements and loss of key committee positions and campaign funding allocations. And the citizens are the losers. The country is not ruled by the wishes of the people but by two competing ideologies that represent polarized conservative and liberal viewpoints.

When one party is in power in both the executive and legislative branches, they have essentially won the game. Unfortunately, those in power are not usually representative of the will of the people or even a large portion of their own party.

My home state of Michigan has become blue turf. The Democrat gang has achieved a stronghold because of two very strong voting blocs: the minority vote and the labor vote. But interestingly, Michigan is, or has been, a very pro-life state. There has been much accomplished to limit abortion and government funding of abortion in our state. But both of our U.S. senators are pro-choice Democrats, and so this pro-life sentiment of our citizens does not carry over to national issues. Our senators are elected in a statewide election but do not represent the will of their constituents on this issue when they travel to Washington. Our state legislators work to stop government funding of abortion at the local level, but our U.S. senators vote to require it at the federal level.

How can this happen? Well, because of current demographics favoring the Democratic Party, the winner of the Democratic primary is sure to be the one elected in a statewide election. And the choice of the Democratic nominee will be skewed by the liberal end of the party. Let's make some assumptions to demonstrate how this can work. Let's assume the following breakdown of voters: Democrats, 40 percent; Republicans, 35 percent; and Independents, 25 percent. Let's further assume the following breakdown of voters with pro-life beliefs: Democrats, 40 percent; Republicans, 80 percent; and

Independents, 50 percent. With these two assumptions, we can demonstrate that even with 56 percent of the voters being pro-life, a pro-choice candidate will be elected on a statewide vote. If everyone sticks with their party and votes with that party's candidate regardless of the voters own positions or views, then our state officials will be determined by whoever can get 50 percent of the Democrat vote in the primary. In other words, the selection of our U. S. senators and our governor is effectively controlled by 20 percent of our population.

We need to look again at our political process, especially the primary system and the Electoral College. A red voter in a blue state effectively has no vote, nor does a blue voter in a red state; they can't vote for purple. Their only avenue to make an impact on the election is to crossover in the primary to try to influence a lighter-shade candidate in the other party, but then they give up their ability to influence local races and issues within their own party. Maybe we need two different primaries; one for national offices and statewide offices and one for local offices. Maybe we need open primaries more like the general elections where we can split our ticket and vote for one party's candidate for U.S. senate and another party's for state senate. Maybe we need some national primary system not split by party at all that could result in the possibility of two politicians from the same party ultimately running against each other for a plurality of the vote.

I am not a political science expert, and revamping our political process is not within the scope of this book, but I do believe strongly that something needs to change in our political system to allow good ideas to surface in Washington. Too many are now screened out by conservative/liberal and Republican/Democrat filters and labels. Our current process is hindering the ability of our nation to act like grownups. It is interfering with our ability to determine what our country ought to do.

If it is not clear by now, the abortion issue is, for me, an unacceptable difference. I cannot, in good conscience, vote for a pro-choice candidate. Unfortunately, this essentially limits me to voting only for Republican candidates. And this I find very frustrating. While the Democrat Party supports many issues that I may approve of and prefer, I cannot vote based on these matters because of a single issue that the Democratic Party has chosen to give unwavering support.

I would argue that being pro-life is much more the result of an unacceptable difference than being pro-choice. The position of pro-life voters is based on deep moral convictions, and there is no possibility for compromise. They believe abortion is murder as a moral absolute and will never vote for someone who condones murder; it violates the *Tao*. It is my opinion, however, that the pro-choice voter's motivations are not grounded at the same level and driven with the same intensity. There are some for sure that think it is a matter of fairness and rights, but for them to vote for a pro-life candidate, although a serious compromise of their values, would not represent a violation of their moral fabric or religious beliefs.

Much of the Republican Party's political strength is built upon the backs of those unwilling to compromise on the abortion issue. The GOP knows they have the votes of committed pro-lifers because these voters have nowhere else to go. If the Democratic Party wanted to clean up and once again become the party of the people, all they would have to do is run pro-life candidates for president and for senators and representatives. They would gain much more from defection of current pro-life Republicans than they would lose from defection of pro-choice Democrats. Where would the latter go? If President Obama were a supporter of a culture of life, his election in 2008 would have been a landslide. But then again, he never would have been nominated.

Any major changes to our political systems or election process will be a long time in coming. In the meantime, we can only control our own voting decisions and try to influence others around us. We can take a personal decision to vote for the best candidates regardless of labels. We can address the issue much like my daughter faced her dating dilemma by starting with an examination of two distinctions: *Is it candidate A or not candidate A?* and *Is it candidate B or not candidate B?* We can make our list of requirements and desires for a candidate and examine each against our list. We look first at the show-stopper issues guided by our unacceptable differences, and then at the nice, but not necessary, items. And we sometimes are forced to vote against a candidate that we cannot accept rather than for a candidate we approve.

SUMMARY

It is important to know ourselves and what we believe in; what are those issues and beliefs that we are not willing to compromise. We need to reflect on what labels we put on ourselves and which ones others put on us. How do you perceive yourself and how do others perceive you, and how does it affect how you can work together? Know that labels can be useful at times, but also be cautious of their dangers.

Know what teams you belong to by choice, by requirement, or by default. Determine if there is a basis for putting your faith in those teams. Be willing to try to influence your team if it has gone astray, or, if necessary, to walk away from it.

Above all, treat everyone as individuals. Do not prejudge them, either favorably or unfavorably, based on their associations. And take personal responsibility for your own behavior. Do not simply go with the flow, thinking and acting the way others say you should. Do what you ought to do, not what others want you to do.

ASKING QUESTIONS
(Solve the Problem, Don't Just Treat the Symptom)

My final three years at General Motors were spent in the Specialty Vehicle Activities group, which was part of the product engineering side of the company. In my role in that organization, I was responsible for reviewing the designs of plastic and composite components and recommending materials, processes, and suppliers for the manufacture of those components. These activities often pushed me beyond the limits of my experience and expertise, but since I came with a different perspective from the manufacturing side of the company, I was more knowledgeable on particular issues than others in our group. In these areas, I was, in some respects, H.G. Wells' "one-eyed man in the valley of the blind."

Because we dealt with low-volume specialty models, there was always a high level of importance placed on keeping the investment for our programs as low as possible. If a mold for producing a plastic part cost $200,000, and we were only going to sell a thousand vehicles with that part, then there was a $200 cost associated with every vehicle produced just to recover that tooling purchase. With the many parts required to execute a special-edition vehicle, costs can mount quickly. The price of the vehicle can become prohibitive if costs are not monitored and controlled closely. For this reason, there was an ongoing interest in creatively pursuing investment reductions, and that sometimes involved compromising standard tooling practices. And so, I was often consulted regarding the risks and trade-offs of accepting various tooling shortcut proposals for low-volume manufacture. But, although I came to the group with a manufacturing background, tooling was not my strongest suit.

On one occasion, I was asked to participate in a conference call between our design team, our part supplier, and their mold builder regarding a new rocker panel molding, a large part that runs along the lower side of the vehicle below the doors. The supplier was requesting changes to our part design to simplify the mold construction. We had a concern, however, that this design modification would cause an unacceptable cosmetic defect in the parts and we were resisting the change for quality reasons. I hesitated to be part of the conference because I didn't have a clear understanding of the nuances and intricacies of the particular mold design issue, but my team insisted. And so, I simply started asking questions with the intent of causing the supplier and mold builder to justify the need for the change. Without really knowing what I was talking about, or where the meeting was headed, my series of questions steered us to a solution that kept the mold simple without compromising our part design.

On that day, I realized that the greatest value I brought to the group was not my ability to answer questions but my ability to ask them. With all the information readily at our disposal through the Internet, almost anyone can find the answer to almost any question. The key is knowing what questions should be asked and how to ask them.

In our everyday lives, we sometimes fail to be questioning people. We accept direction and advice from others without asking some basic questions to see if that advice makes sense.

It's important to ask some probing questions to get below the surface to find the truth of what we ought to do. We can ask questions directly of people or we can examine data and analyze test results as ways of answering our queries. In any case, we need to consider some of the concepts that we have already discussed when asking our questions. Particularly, we need to determine whether we can have faith in the sources of our information.

Let's say you go into your living room and find that your once-beautiful, favorite lamp is now broken and lying on the floor. And so you call your children into the room and ask them, "How did this happen?" and, "Who did this?" And you receive a chorus back stating, "I don't know!" and, "It wasn't me." While your children may be technically competent to answer your questions, you may not put a lot of faith in their answers; their truthfulness is in question because of their fear of punishment or of simply losing your favor.

My mom tells the story of my Uncle Joe. When he was young, my grandmother convinced him that she could tell if he was lying by smelling his finger. He confessed a lot of offenses before he figured out she was bluffing all along.

Learning how to read people to determine if they are telling you the truth is probably something that cannot be completely taught. It comes with experience and observations of human nature. This ability might make you a good poker player if you can read signs and reactions that others unconsciously transmit. But there are some techniques that can be learned and applied to determine if you have faithful sources of data for making good decisions.

Asking something you already know: Pocket calculators are commonplace today; they're even built into our phones. But I can remember when they first came on the scene and can recall the doubts that we, as early users, had in accepting the results they provided us. What was the first thing we did when we got our first calculator? We multiplied three times four to check and make sure it gave us what we already knew was the correct answer, twelve. And in the classroom, when we took our first tests using the calculator to replace our slide rules, we would double check the answers with our slide rules, or even with long-hand calculations, if we had sufficient time. Only after we had developed a history of answers that we knew to be correct did we finally put our faith in the calculator. We use the same technique in the laboratory for calibrating equipment or evaluating procedures with known samples or conditions. For example, if we doubt the performance of a thermometer, we can get a quick assessment of its accuracy by checking the readings it provides in ice water and in boiling water to see if we obtain thirty-two degrees Fahrenheit and two hundred and twelve degrees Fahrenheit, respectively.

But we can also use this same technique with people. We can test someone's truthfulness and competence by asking questions of them to which we already know the answers. It is best, if possible, to ask questions that will require that a truthful response might also be to the responder's disadvantage. In this way, you can get a read not only on their competence but also on their honesty at the same time. For example, you might be trying to select a new financial advisor. Hopefully, that person will know much more about investing than you do, but you need to do enough homework so that you can challenge him and find out if he is both knowledgeable and honest. And you can do this by taking one very specific issue and conducting some research so that you know that issue very well. It might be the subject of annuities, for example. You can then pose some questions to your prospective advisor about trade-offs with annuities and when they should be included in your portfolio and when they don't make sense. If his answers honestly and objectively match with what you already know to be true, then you can probably also trust him with matters on which you are not as knowledgeable. If his answers are incorrect, and slanted toward a product that he is clearly promoting, then it is time to move on to the next candidate.

Making statements which are incorrect: This technique is a little more subtle and requires that you be confident with who you are, because it basically requires you to pretend to be ignorant. You do this to see if the other person is competent enough to notice and honest enough to inform you of your errors. My wife and I inadvertently used this technique a few years back. We were picking out ceramic tiles for a bathroom remodeling project, and our tile contractor gave us several options of salesrooms to visit. On our visit to the first store, we were given a short discussion of the tile choices and then left alone to compare the different styles and colors and materials. We struggled with all the choices, and we were in the process of evaluating a tile for the floor and a tile for the wall, which were from the same manufacturer but from different product series; they obviously didn't match well. It was at this time that our salesperson returned, and she cheerfully complemented us on what she thought was our selection. We moved on to the next store very quickly.

Asking multiple sources: When our doctor gives us a diagnosis of a serious illness, or the need for a major surgery, we immediately want a second opinion. We may have had blind trust in that same doctor to take care of our health and treat everyday illnesses, but suddenly we have questions about his competence. It is a good thing for our own well-being to seek a second opinion regarding serious medical procedures, and most insurance companies require it for their own protection as well.

We get multiple opinions in many aspects of our lives. We get a more accurate estimate of the cost of a new car or a new roof on the house when we solicit multiple quotes. And today, the ability to conduct online searches makes comparative shopping a lot more convenient than in the past.

In industry, it is good practice not to conduct an experiment with only one test sample. Multiple tests are run, sometimes at different laboratories, to increase the confidence that the answers that the data provide will truthfully answer the questions that motivated the test.

In all these ways, we effectively ask a question of multiple sources to obtain the most reliable answer. It is a tool, however, that we often ignore when making some of the more serious decision in our lives. We are sometimes afraid or too proud to ask advice from many sources who could provide us with reliable information and offer a different perspective. There was one gentleman I worked with who came at most situations from a different perspective than I did, but we respected each other for our technical knowledge. I would ask for his opinion, although I would almost never follow his suggestion, because it was often useful to factor in his considerations and viewpoints into the decision-making process. He asked for my opinions in much the same way. We have to be careful of only asking people who will tell us what we want to hear.

Making contact: With all the computers and electronic communication capability available to us, there can be the danger of losing sight of the value of face-to-face communications. We can see it in the home where people lock themselves away on the computer and do not interact with other family members and family members text each other instead of calling and talking with them directly. In the workplace, I have seen coop students and young engineers get lost in their cubicles, hiding behind their computer screens, not willing to venture out on the shop floor to learn the valuable lessons that can only be taught by human interactions. During a protracted troubleshooting project, I chose to drive 500 miles every Friday to lead a two-hour meeting with three of our suppliers because it was so much more productive and fruitful than when I attempted to conduct the meeting remotely on a conference call. Too many misunderstandings resulted over the phone without the non-verbal cues to keep us out of trouble.

What would you do? This simple question, especially when addressed face-to-face, can be very disarming and appeals to the responder's basic desire to want to do the right thing. When I travelled a fair amount for my job, the question at the end of the day when we got to the hotel was where to go for dinner. And if I asked the receptionist at the front desk, she always had a list of recommended restaurants provided by the hotel management; the local pizzeria or steakhouse might even have an advertisement printed on the room keycard. But I found I could get a better recommendation by asking the receptionist where she went for pizza or for Chinese or Mexican food. She would honestly give her opinion of the best places to eat; partly because she was glad that I valued her opinion and partly because she knew she would have to face me when I returned from my meal.

And when the construction crew was working on replacing the shingles on my roof, there was the chance that some of the plywood sheathing may need to be replaced as well. I made a point of talking directly to the workers, looking them in the eye, and asking them to treat my home as if it were their own. If there was a question whether a sheet of plywood should be replaced or not, I asked them to decide the same way as they would if this were their own house.

So far I have discussed some techniques that may be useful for improving our chances of getting good answers to our questions. I would now like to discuss some problem-solving strategies that can help guide us to know what questions to ask.

RED X

Our children had a game that we still play with our granddaughter. It's a two-player game called "Guess Who?" by Milton Bradley. Each player has a board in front of them with pictures of twenty-four different characters. The players each pick a card representing one of the characters without disclosing it to their opponent. The object of the game is to determine which character is on your opponent's card. The two players alternate asking yes/no questions of their opponent, trying to zero-in on the character's identity by process of elimination. Since the questions are of the yes/no variety, they are effectively questions of distinction. For example, a question may be: *Is your character a male?* Depending on the answer to the question, a number of possibilities will be eliminated. One of the strategies of the game is to try to ask the most valuable questions, the questions that can eliminate the most pictures in front of you. The game is set up, however, to make this difficult. Most of the distinctions are set up on a 5:19 split. For example, five of the characters are female and nineteen are male, five have glasses, five have hats, five have mustaches, five are blonds, five are redheads, five have white hair, and five are bald. If our starting question of the game is based on any of these distinctions, there will be a five in twenty-four chance of eliminating nineteen characters from consideration if the character has that feature, and a nineteen in twenty-four chance that only five will be eliminated if the character does not have the feature. With a few calculations, we can determine that, on average, about eight of the twenty-four characters would be eliminated using one of these questions. Without any deep analysis such as this, however, it was interesting to see how quickly the kids intuitively picked up on this importance of asking good questions. I mentioned that there are five characters with mustaches, but there are also four with beards and one that has both a beard and mustache. There are eight, therefore, that have at least one of these two features. The starting question often became: *Does your character have facial hair?* With this question, there is an eight out of twenty-four chance of the character having facial hair, and thus eliminating sixteen characters, and a sixteen out of twenty-four chance of eliminating only eight characters if he does not. On average, about eleven characters will be eliminated with this question. It is a much more valuable question to ask than: *Does your character wear glasses?*

Asking the most valuable questions is one of the key strategies to the *Red X* problem-solving technique used in industry. In this approach, problem solvers are taught to try to zero in on the location of the cause of a problem by asking questions that narrow down the possibilities as rapidly as possible. They call it splitting the dictionary and use a training exercise in which a person is asked to think of a word. The solver then opens a dictionary to the middle, looks at the first word on that page, and asks if the unknown word comes before or after that word alphabetically. Depending on the answer, the solver then splits the dictionary once again and repeats the process until the page containing the unknown word is determined. And then it is simply a matter of splitting the page down in a similar fashion. The claim is that with this technique, any word can be determined using a standard dictionary by asking no more than twenty questions. The 10th *Edition Merriam-Webster Collegiate Dictionary* has about 160,000 entries on 1,375 pages, or on average, about 120 entries per page. By the splitting the dictionary, we should be able to determine the correct page in about eleven splits and identify the correct word on that page in around another seven splits.

The *Red X* strategy can have some practical applications in diagnosing problems with vehicles, appliances around the house, or even our own health. If a lamp doesn't work, for example, you might start by doing a test, essentially asking a question, to determine whether the problem is in the lamp or in the power supply. And you can conduct a simple test to determine the answer by plugging the lamp into a known good outlet, one where another lamp is currently functioning properly. If the lamp still does not work, then you may exchange the light bulb to determine if the problem is in the lamp or in the bulb. By a few simple tests, you can isolate the location of the problem, and then identifying the cause is much easier.

One of the keys to the success of the *Red X* strategy is that it requires that questions be asked on the basis of distinctions. For example, one might ask: *Is a defect present in the part at a particular point in a process or not?* or, *Does the defect always occur at the same location on the part or is it random?* In this way, you can always be sure of what you know. In many less-disciplined approaches to problem solving, there is a tendency to ask questions in a way that results in subjective responses; the answers are not clear. Based on their previous experience, the researchers often interpret these answers and develop what they *think* they know about the problem. There is a tendency to jump to conclusions, ruling out valid possibilities and concentrating on making false ones fit their preconceived idea of the situation.

Often in our lives we jump at bits of information that agree with our own vision of an issue without fully testing their validity. We react to anecdotal stories and assume that the lessons and facts that they describe are universally applicable. And we end up thinking we know more than we actually do. What we have, instead, are opinions. They may be true, but we cannot be sure, and so we must be careful about what decisions we make based on our questionable database.

When faced with difficult choices, start by determining what information is needed to confidently make your important decisions. Then develop a questioning strategy that will give you objective answers that you can trust; information that you will know to be true, not that you will believe might be true.

FIVE WHYS

Small children are naturally curious, and they all seem to go through that stage when they drive their parents crazy by repeatedly asking, "Why?" Sometimes we wonder if they really want answers or just attention. We often struggle to know the answers ourselves and struggle even more to put the answers in a form understandable to a three-year-old. Our reward for this effort is simply their wide-eyed response as they ask again, "Why?" We get frustrated because the questions never seem to stop.

This repeated questioning reminds me of another problem-solving method referred to as the *Five Whys,* which is often used in industry to try to get at the root cause of a problem. It can be particularly useful when investigating injuries that result from accidents in the workplace to make sure that the corrective actions, which are put in place following an incident, will be effective in preventing a reoccurrence. The method involves asking a series of *why* questions which are aimed at finding the cause of the problem. The goal is to avoid being distracted by the symptoms. There is no magic to the number five; sometimes it will take more than five questions, sometimes less. And sometimes there will be multiple answers to one *why* question which can lead to alternative solutions. The point is to be inquisitive and to keep digging to find the true source of a problem, to act with the persistence of a three-year-old. It helps to clear our vision to see what ought to be done.

As an example, suppose my mother came to visit at my home and she fell on my driveway. (This didn't really happen.) I can try to determine why this accident occurred.

Q: Why did my mother fall on the driveway?
A: *She slipped on the ice that was on the driveway.*

Without trying to assess the situation any further, I could develop the following list of possible solutions:

- Provide my mother with a set of crampons so that she can walk safely on ice. (In industry, we refer to this as supplying her with the appropriate PPE, personal protective equipment.)
- Monitor the driveway for ice and apply salt, as required, to melt the ice.
- Forbid my mother from visiting during the winter.
- Instruct my mother to approach the house by the sidewalk to the front door, thus avoiding the driveway.
- Determine when my mother will be arriving and meet her at the base of the driveway to provide her assistance.

But by asking a few more *why* questions, we can try to get at the root cause of the problem:

Q: Why was there ice on the driveway?
A: *Because water from the downspout refroze there.*

Q: Why was water from the downspout flowing down the driveway?
A: *Because the downspout was routed improperly.*

With these two additional questions, we can see that the real solution is to reroute the downspout so that water melting on the roof is not deposited where it can refreeze on a surface where people are expected to walk. This may be a simplistic example, but hopefully it illustrates the importance of asking *why* questions. I'm sure that, without expending very much energy, you can come up with a list of problems around your own house that may be similar; conditions where you manage a symptom rather than addressing the true problem.

Or maybe there is a problem in your relationship with your spouse and you might prevent fights and arguments by trying to avoid the real issues. Or maybe there is a discipline problem with a child, and you address his actions but not the reasons for his actions. In both cases, you are, in effect, treating and controlling the symptoms. Unless the root cause of the problem is determined and addressed, the problems in the relationships will continue to manifest themselves and unhealthy resentments will grow.

I have already mentioned that in the *Five Whys* approach, there is the possibility of more than one answer to any of the *why* questions. Instead of a linear result to the questioning, branching may occur that can lead to alternative solutions. There are often multiple approaches that can be taken; we then have options to compare to determine the most practical solution.

In the last chapter, I mentioned the poverty that I witnessed in Haiti. People are living in tin box houses surrounded by their own sewage with no clean water for drinking or bathing, and they are hungry. We can look for the cause of the hunger.

Q: Why is the family hungry?
A: *They have no food.*

If we stop at the answer to this first why question, the solution is to solicit donations of food. But it treats only the symptom of the problem; the people will be hungry again tomorrow. So we can ask another question which can be answered in two different ways.

Q: Why don't they have food?
A: *They don't have equipment, supplies, or training to grow crops, raise livestock, or catch fish.*
Q: Why don't they have equipment or training?
A: *They don't have money, and there is no training available.*

If we follow this chain of questioning, the solution might be to solicit donations to buy boats and farm equipment and chickens and sheep and seeds and provide the people with training so that they can be self-sufficient and live off the land. Or we can back up and answer in a different way.

Q: Why don't they have food?
A: *The family doesn't have any money to buy food.*

Q: Why doesn't the family have any money?
A: *Because the father doesn't have a job.*

Q: Why doesn't he have a job?
A: *Because the unemployment rate is 50 percent, and because he has no job skills.*

Q: Why is the unemployment rate so high?
A: *Because government policies, political unrest, and violence have driven away the once thriving tourist industry and new industry is reluctant to locate there.*

If we follow this chain of questioning, we might be led to pursue political and industrial solutions.

With this simple analysis, we can demonstrate how different solutions can be developed. The correct answer is probably a balanced combination of all three solutions but possibly addressed by completely different organizations. Relief organizations, for example, must be careful to steer clear of any political activism or they will risk losing their freedom to carry out their charitable efforts. Different groups can have the common objective of eliminating hunger, but use different means to attain that goal. And yet they are working together.

It is important to ask questions to know what you ought to do based on your individual talents and resources and not feel obligated to do what someone else wants you to do.

We can also look at many aspects of the abortion issue by asking *why* questions. It can lead us to some better understandings of the true concerns behind our differences and can provide some insights on how to address the situation more effectively and productively. We can try to understand each other better by asking why someone is pro-life, why someone is pro-choice, or why someone is pro-abortion. We can ask *why* questions to try to determine the reasons why a mother chooses the option of abortion and not the option of adoption or the option of raising the child herself. We can ask *why* questions to determine the reasons a mother conceived a child that was unwanted. These are all simple lines of questioning that can point to different forms of solutions to resolving conflicts. The answers can guide us in determining what it is we ought to do. But these questions are rarely asked.

Years ago, when I first began to be active in pro-life activities, I did what I often do when I chase after a new pursuit; I acted without fully thinking things through. I acted based on my tendencies to simplify a situation by applying labels and putting things (and people) into categories as I cautioned against in the last chapter. In this case, I had already developed my stereotypical image of someone who is pro-choice. And so when I was leafing through a pro-life magazine, trying to become better informed and enlightened on how I could contribute to the cause, I ran across an ad for a T-shirt. The T-shirt had a question and two pictures. The question was: *Are you pro-choice?* The first picture was of a baby carriage with the arm of a baby visibly protruding from the top. It was labeled *choice A*. The second picture was of a trash can with the same baby's arm protruding from the top. It was labeled *choice B*. I immediately got out my checkbook and sent off an order.

The next day, I was having a pro-life discussion at work and proudly mentioned the shirt I had ordered. One of my co-workers gave me a look of disgust. I was asked what was going to happen if abortion was once again illegal. How was society, how was the Church, going to change to embrace women with unplanned pregnancies in a more compassionate way so that they didn't feel trapped into what they often felt was the only way out?

That short conversation, or should I say rebuke, sent me back to read some more and try to clarify my thoughts on my pro-life activities. And I stumbled upon a book by David Reardon, *The Jericho Plan*. And in his book, the author makes the claim that we all know someone who has had an abortion. I stopped in mid-sentence and decided that he must be wrong because, at that time, I didn't know anyone. But then he continued, "Even if their abortions have been kept a secret from us." And then reading another book at the time, I discovered that in the mid-1980s about thirty percent of all pregnancies in the U.S. ended in abortion. In other words, about one out of every three babies that was conceived ended up being aborted. (Fortunately that number is coming down, but in 2005 it was still at about twenty-five percent. That is, for every three babies born, one is aborted.) I knew the mothers of many babies that had been born; I surely must have known the mothers of many babies who were not. I just didn't know who they were. I mentioned this in a homily one Sunday and I received a beautiful and courageous letter from a parishioner the next week. She identified herself as one of those mothers that I knew who had had an abortion. She talked about the pain and the regrets, how it ruined her relationship with the father of that aborted child, how she could never do it again but how she didn't feel she had a choice at the time.

It became clear to me that to make a contribution to the effort to put an end to abortion, I must start by trying to understand why so many mothers, so many women that I know, make the choice that they do. And I went back to Reardon's book and read this claim, "Over 70 percent of women undergoing abortion believe it is morally wrong. They are acting *against* their conscience because they feel they have no other choice." Reardon cited Federica Mathewes-Green who stated, "No woman wants an abortion as she wants an ice cream cone or a Porsche. She wants an abortion as an animal caught in a trap wants to gnaw off its own leg." For many, abortion is an act of despair when no other choice appears to exist.

I learned a lot from my investigation of questions others had already asked. I came to understand that there is no stereotypical pro-choice person. Some claim to be pro-choice because to do otherwise would be a judgment or condemnation on a close friend or family member who was trapped into a decision to abort. There are a lot of women who I meet every day or pass on the street who have had abortions that I don't know about. And so, by the time my shirt arrived in the mail, I had already decided that I could never wear it. It poses a good question, but not in a very loving and productive way.

When a woman is faced with an unwanted pregnancy, she has three choices today. She can have the baby and raise it herself, have the baby and place it for adoption, or have an abortion. This is where most of the abortion discussions begin. But in doing so, we are dealing with a symptom of the problem and not its root cause. We can also pursue a line of questioning that attempts to determine why there is an unwanted pregnancy. To address this question, I would like to utilize a different tool, the flow chart, to better map out and illustrate the possibilities.

FLOW CHARTS

Engineers who design processes or control circuits often start with a flow diagram or flow chart. It describes how the desired systems should function and is the outline for laying out equipment or programming logic circuits. Flow charts are also used as a method of troubleshooting a problem. If we are having a problem with our computer or water softener or car, we can refer to the owner's manual and be guided through a series of questions that lead us through a decision tree that direct us to the cause of our problem, and hopefully the solution. In effect, these troubleshooting guides are an embodiment and formalization of the *Red X* strategies. Flow charts can also be used to reverse engineer the design of a process or product and help to better understand how it works.

One of the beauties of flow charts is that their pictorial nature can make a very complex problem much more easily understood and evaluated. We don't have to keep a lot of issues and concerns organized in our heads. They are also based on binary, yes/no, responses that help to avoid gray areas and force agreements to be reached. Flow charts can also provide a useful structure for examining the impact of alternative solutions.

I have included a flow diagram that tries to capture the decisions that may be made in response to a sexual stimulation and desire for sexual release. The diagram is, in itself, made up of a series of questions, but we can stop at each individual step of the diagram and ask an additional series of questions to probe the factors behind the decision process. We can also examine how these factors have changed over time and how the outcomes may be different if conditions were changed.

For example, if we look at Box 1 in our diagram, we can ask questions about the sources of sexual stimulation and examine how they have changed over time in our society. And I think everyone can agree that the occasions for exposure to sexual stimuli are much greater than they were fifty years ago in our culture. This results from relaxed standards for prime time television shows and commercials, immodest fashions, strong and explicit sexual content in mainstream movies, explicit music lyrics, and, of course, the readily available nudity and pornography present on the Internet.

We can also examine the filter provided by Box 2 to see if societal norms have affected whether we repress or express our sexual desires. And again, I believe that there would be general agreement that the balance of this decision has also shifted dramatically over the years. The moral code once taught in the family and in church and in school has been replaced by society's attitude that says if it feels good, do it. Flawed research studies by Kinsey were used to argue against sexual continence because it was unnatural and unhealthy. Expressions of sexuality which were once considered taboo, contained in Boxes 5, 7, and 9, are now given wider social acceptability. For example, masturbation is represented by Box 5. In 1994, Jocelyn Elders, the U.S. Surgeon General, commented about masturbation, "I think that it is part of human sexuality, and perhaps it should be taught." Times have changed.

Widespread access to new forms of contraception, and to abortion, have made one of the consequences of sexual activity of less concern. All in all, I think it is pretty clear that by reflecting briefly on changes in our society, we can see that the number of *yes* responses exiting Box 2 today is much greater than it would have been fifty or a hundred years ago.

If we look at the question posed in Box 10, we can consider how all Christian denominations taught against contraception for the first 1,900 years of Christianity. It was only in 1930 that

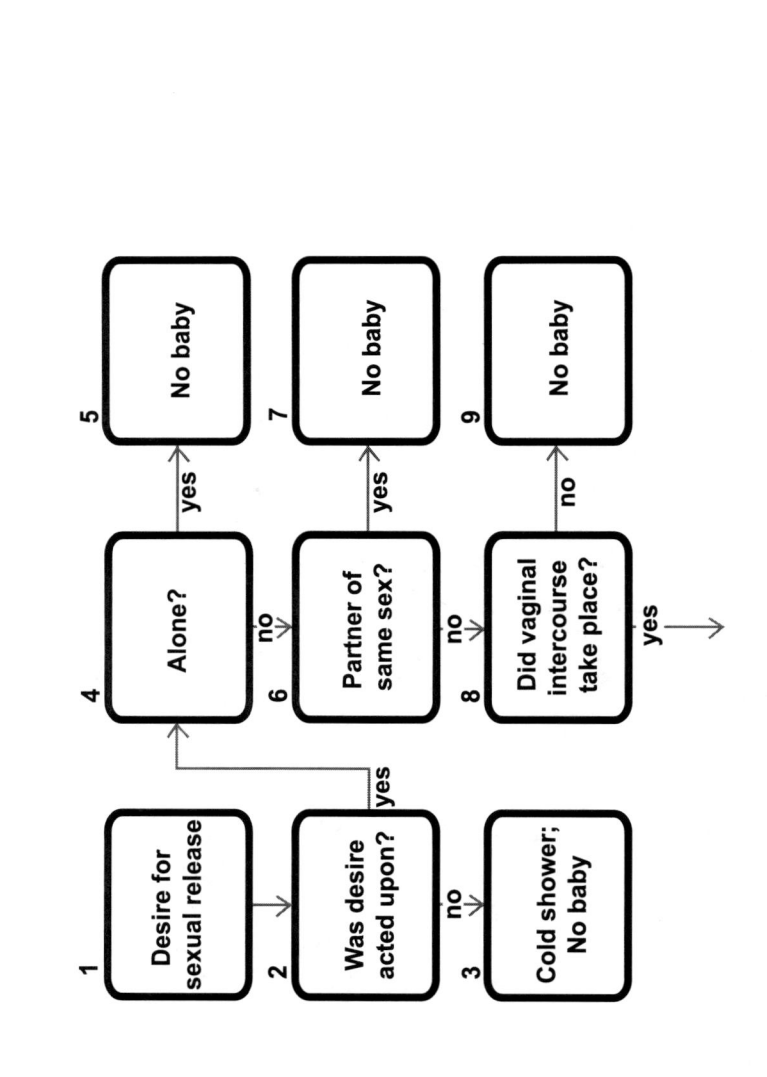

```
1. Desire for sexual release
   → 2. Was desire acted upon?
      — no → 3. Cold shower; No baby
      — yes → 4. Alone?
         — yes → 5. No baby
         — no → 6. Partner of same sex?
            — yes → 7. No baby
            — no → 8. Did vaginal intercourse take place?
               — no → 9. No baby
               — yes →
```

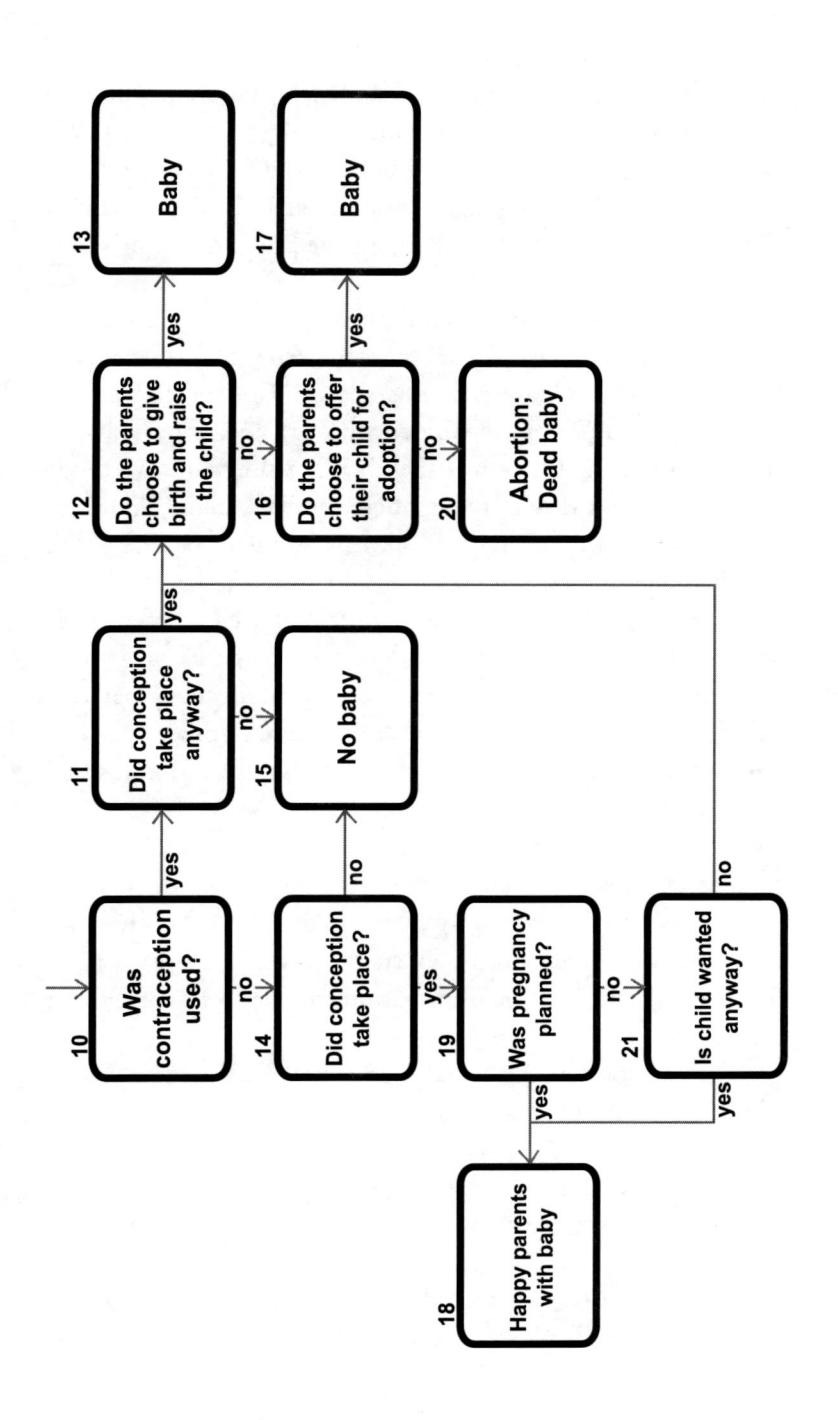

```
10. Was contraception used?
    — yes → 11. Did conception take place anyway?
        — yes → 12. Do the parents choose to give birth and raise the child?
            — yes → 13. Baby
            — no → 16. Do the parents choose to offer their child for adoption?
                — yes → 17. Baby
                — no → 20. Abortion; Dead baby
        — no → 15. No baby
    — no → 14. Did conception take place?
        — yes → 19. Was pregnancy planned?
            — yes → 18. Happy parents with baby
            — no → 21. Is child wanted anyway?
                — yes → 18. Happy parents with baby
                — no → 12. Do the parents choose to give birth and raise the child?
        — no → 15. No baby
```

the Anglican Church at their Lambeth Conference opened the door to changing this previously universal teaching. We can ask questions to probe and understand why the teaching was changed. Was it changed because what Christians ought to do had changed? Or did it change because what Christians wanted to do had changed?

We can look at Box 11 and ask why contraception methods fail. We can consider that statistics from the Guttmacher Institute and the Centers for Disease Control and Prevention indicate that 54 percent of women who had abortions had used contraception in the month they became pregnant. Methods of contraception vary in their inherent effectiveness, and their rates of failure will often be dependent on the discipline of the couple. Condom use, for example, is reported to be 85–98 percent effective as a means of birth control. If used perfectly over the course of a year, 2 percent of couples will conceive a child. For typical use, however, that number can rise to 15 percent. Planned Parenthood tells teens the 2 percent number. One can only wonder about the actual effectiveness of condom use by teenagers in the back seat of a car.

We can look at Boxes 12 and 16 and try to understand why couples faced with an unwanted pregnancy make the choices they do. We can ask why only 2 percent of babies conceived are adopted, but 25 percent are aborted. How can we learn from the answers and use this information we obtain to change the balance?

We can look at the racial inequalities in Box 20 and ask why 42 percent of black babies are aborted but only 15 percent of non-Hispanic, white babies are aborted. What decision factors are different in the flow diagram for black couples and white couples? How can we use this information to stop the killing of black babies at such an inordinate rate?

We can try to understand what resources would need to be put in place if abortion were made illegal. How many of the over one million babies currently aborted each year would be raised by the parent(s), and how many would be placed for adoption? How would society and government need to adapt to these changes? Would the number of unwanted babies go down through increased abstinence or more disciplined contraception use, if couples knew that abortion was no longer available as a back-up method of family planning?

Obviously, there are many more strategic and valuable questions we can ask. It is not the intention here, however, to solve the abortion controversy, but to demonstrate the value of asking good questions to shed light on a very complex issue and to break down barriers to dialogue; to determine what we ought to do working together.

SUMMARY

Being people who ask questions is important for making good choices on our life journey. We need to seek out reliable sources of information and determine whom we should trust. We need to obtain information from multiple sources so that we can better grasp multi-faceted issues that we face along the way. As philosophers, we realize that we cannot know all things and must always retain a questioning nature to help us grow in understanding. We can interact better with others when we try to understand their perspective. And this will help all to see what ought to be done and why.

By asking questions, we are more likely to be perceived by others as open-minded, and we can use this to build bridges and promote open discussions of sensitive issues. But it is important to be sincere and not hypocritical. Do not feign openness and then ask trick questions to try to trap the responder. This will build walls instead of bridges.

WE'RE ALL IN THIS TOGETHER
(Be Tour Guides Now or Submarine Captains Later)

On April 23, 1964, Ken Johnson of the Houston Colt .45s (now the Astros) went to the mound to face the Cincinnati Reds. All of his pitches were working that night, and he went on to pitch a no-hitter, one of those rare accomplishments for a major league pitcher. It was a great personal achievement, but unfortunately, because of two errors in the ninth inning, the Colt .45s lost by a score of 1–0 that night.

In professional sports, we encounter many occasions when an impressive individual performance goes for naught. We feel a bit sad for the player who cannot properly celebrate his accomplishment because it occurred in a losing effort.

And life can be considered much like a team sport. It is difficult to celebrate our personal victories when our friends, family, and community are not sharing in our success; when we are not winning as a team. We are all in this game of life together; we should all be on the same team striving to reach our goal.

And so we need to reflect on what impact our individual actions, or inactions, have on steering society on the right paths to a winning destination. Do we choose the right paths ourselves or do we go along with the crowd, and in so doing, lead others astray as well? And if we seek out the straight path and try to follow it, do we do it alone or do we encourage others to walk along with us? I would contend that the latter option is the only one that will help heal our society. If we are silent, we may pitch a no-hitter and find our own way to heaven. But what will happen if our team still loses? What about our teammates, especially our children and grandchildren?

FIGHTING THE HERD MENTALITY

Here are three interesting quotes for consideration. The first comes from the Old Testament:

> Neither shall you allege the example of the many as an excuse for doing wrong.
>
> Exodus 23:2

The second comes from the philosopher Augustine:

> Wrong is wrong, even if everyone else is doing it. Right is right, even if no one else is doing it.
>
> St. Augustine

And the third quote is from my father. I remember first hearing it about fifty years ago.

> If everyone else jumped off the bridge, would you jump off the bridge too?
>
> Joseph Hulway, Sr.

This question came from my father when I was probably about eight years old. I wanted to wear an inappropriate shirt to school and defended my decision with the common claim: "Everyone else is doing it." My father taught me an early lesson about not succumbing to the herd mentality. How often this lesson can be tested on our journeys when others are cheating on their taxes, when others are being promiscuous, when others are stealing supplies from work, when others are using alcohol or drugs illegally or abusively, or when others don't go to church on Sunday. Often, what others are doing is a lot more attractive or convenient than what we know deep down we ought to do.

I was blessed with loving parents who were willing to be parents. Too often today, however, mothers and fathers are instead more concerned with being friends to their children and they abdicate their responsibility to teach the discipline needed for their children's futures. For most in my generation, our parents were role models for how to act as adults. Now, unfortunately, many parents don't act like adults; they'd rather follow their children and look to them as role models on how to be teenagers. I think our society is becoming stuck in its adolescence because many of our adults are afraid of growing up.

It is my opinion that some of the adults don't want to grow up because they have lost their confidence and hope about what exists at the end of their journey; they fight to stay young and enjoy the journey for as long as possible. And their children can become lost as a result.

For our thirtieth wedding anniversary, my wife and I took a trip to an all-inclusive resort just outside of Cancun. When we were at the airport waiting for our plane to depart from Detroit, we observed a couple with their two teenage daughters waiting to board the same charter. Based on their comments and actions, and their tattoos, I would guess the girls' ages at about fifteen and seventeen. A week later, after a beautiful and relaxing trip, we bumped into the same family on the shuttle bus taking us to the remote parking facility and could not help but overhear stories of their adventures. It turns out that the teens stayed at a completely different resort than the parents. The parents apparently placed their own freedom and independence ahead of the welfare of their girls. We were aghast as we listened to the daughters recount stories of late-night adventures, but their *parents* were amused. They shared together as if they were a group of teenage friends.

Some parents find it easier to go with the flow and do not want to upset their children. They want to be friends to their children and not parents. I know of many parents who disagree with their children's decision to move in with their boyfriend or girlfriend but then facilitate and indirectly condone the behavior. They physically help pack and move boxes. They visit with the cohabitating couple and act as if nothing is wrong. They don't want to be considered judgmental.

FOLLOWING THE PATH WE SEE

I met a young lady on a pilgrimage to the Holy Land, and she shared a little with me of her conversion story. She had led quite a wild and exciting life filled with excesses and inappropriate behavior before ultimately falling on her knees in prayer; turning to God in desperation at the emptiness of her life. She had a dramatic conversion which she attributed primarily to the prayers of her mother, and she chose to move into the light. I don't remember many of the details of her story, but what does remain with me clearly is her admission of her ongoing struggle. She confided to me, "There are still times when I just want to be bad." Following the straight path is not always easy. When I think about her story, I am reminded of my own daily struggles to stay on the straight path. And I take comfort in knowing that St. Paul also fought a continual battle.

> What I do, I do not understand. For I do not do what I want, but I do what I hate. Now if I do

what I do not want, I concur that the law is good. So now it is no longer I who do it, but sin that dwells in me. For I know that good does not dwell in me, that is, in my flesh. The willing is ready at hand, but doing the good is not. For I do not do the good I want, but I do the evil I do not want. Now if (I) do what I do not want, it is no longer I who do it, but sin that dwells in me.

Romans 7:15–20

We can recognize the *Tao* as being good, yet still stumble along the path because sometimes having fun today is a lot more attractive than contemplating long-term happiness; and so we take a few wrong turns because, although our spirit is willing, our flesh is weak. We are sinners and we fail, but the good news is that if we know we are weak and admit that we are lost and not following the right path, we can turn on our GPS and recalculate a new course to get us heading back in the right direction.

Even when we have clear vision and identify the right path, life will still be a struggle to follow that path. But it is a battle we can win with God's help and his endless forgiveness. But what about those who do not know or admit that they are lost? They will not find the way without our help. Are we willing to offer help and guidance, to be tour guides to help others find the right path and point out those that lead to danger? Will others listen to our advice?

When I was young, if I misbehaved or did something wrong down the street or on the next block, my parents would somehow find out about it. Neighbors were closer and often relatives lived nearby as well. The village didn't raise me, but it sure was willing to provide strategic intelligence to my parents so they would be equipped to do the best job possible.

But I believe we have lost this sense of looking out for others and trying to prevent them from going astray. There is a higher level of isolationism, a desire to mind our own business and not to get involved. And, from a selfish perspective, that might be a fine approach if our futures as individuals were independent of the future of the world around us. But that, of course, is clearly not the case. We need to take part in shaping the society around us. We cannot just worry about what we ought to do; we need to try to help others determine what they ought to do as well.

TOUR GUIDES

On a hiking trip a few years back, my wife and I trekked four miles into Johns Brook Lodge, a rustic facility at the heart of the Adirondack High Peak region in New York State. On the third day there, my wife was unable to join me on the day's hike because of muscle cramps in her legs. Two women we met at dinner the night before sensed that I was on my own for the day and invited me to accompany them on their trip up Gothics. Since Gothics is one of my favorite mountains, I readily accepted. My new hiking companions took turns leading us along the path, and I followed quietly behind, thankful for the company and not wanting to be an imposition. For a portion of our journey, the trail crisscrossed and followed up a small stream. As the two women talked and picked their way along the rocks and roots of the stream, however, they failed to notice that the path veered off to the right and headed away from the stream and into the woods; it is sometimes easy to lose the way even on a well-travelled route, especially when the way ahead looks like a clear path. Fortunately, I noticed where the path changed direction and stopped so that they did not lead me astray. I let them proceed a short way ahead in the wrong direction before I called out to them, and they hiked back to me so that we could start off together along the way we ought to go. They realized they had made a mistake and were more than willing to accept my course correction because they knew it would help them get to their destination safely that day.

Sometimes we encounter people who make wrong turns in life because they are careless; their vision is distracted from seeing the correct way to travel. And on those occasions, they are thankful for some words of guidance and direction. But often, on our journey through life, our guidance and counsel are rejected and we are rebuffed. We are accused of being critical and judgmental. On matters dealing with especially sensitive issues, we can even be accused of hate speech for trying to point out that others are taking a dangerous path that may not lead them to the right destination, to the place they hope to be at the end of their time on earth. And I anticipate that one day I will be fined or imprisoned myself for views I express from the pulpit which will be labeled as hate speech.

Plato said, "We can easily forgive a child who is afraid of the dark; the real tragedy of life is when men are afraid of the light." It is indeed a tragedy when adults want to stay in the dark and not admit to the light of truth. It is tragic because of the impact on themselves, but even more tragic because of the impact on those who look to them as role models and guides.

If we do not know that we are lost, we will not ask for or accept directions from people who may be able to provide us with guidance. And one of the biggest problems in our society is that many are not willing to admit that they are lost. They do not recognize that there are things that they ought to do and things that they ought not do. When we know we are lost, we look at a map, but when we do not know we are lost, we disregard maps and ignore our guidance systems. When we sin we can ask for God's forgiveness and try to correct our path, but what happens when we lose comprehension that sin even exists?

I mentioned in the introduction that this book presupposes that the reader has a belief in God. I've seen surveys that indicate that 95 percent of those in our country claim to have that belief, but it is difficult to determine how many hold that belief with a strong level of faith. For many, it seems that it is simply lip service, the appropriate thing to say. The actions of our culture betray the reality that we are becoming more of a godless nation and world. We look at what others do to determine what is acceptable for us, and do not look to what our Creator says we ought to do. We follow and trust others who are also lost, and we can find ourselves following them as they jump off the bridge.

As parents, as members of society, it is our duty to offer instruction and share our knowledge of what is right and wrong, of what we ought to do and what we ought not do. We need to help others find objective truths about the world around us. This is not being judgmental, it is being loving. We care about the decisions others make because we care about the destinations to which their paths will lead them. But, in the end, we have no ability to take away their freedom to make choices for themselves.

We are careful not to judge others because of what they do because we cannot know what is in their mind and heart, but we can be clear about stating objectively the appropriateness of the actions they choose. We can objectively define sinful behavior, but we cannot accuse someone else of being a sinner. And we cannot judge others because we ourselves are sinners.

As our society drifts away from its focus on God, its citizens are becoming more and more amoral; they no longer are in touch with the *Tao*. And we can reflect on whether an amoral person can perform an immoral act. Society's legal system has a principle that ignorance of the law is not a valid defense. How will God's system of justice rule on this matter? We don't know for sure, but I'm pretty sure we will have some culpability for intentionally allowing ourselves to stay in a state of ignorance. We will also probably be culpable for not trying to help others to know the truth and, in so doing, leading them astray. The evangelist Luke recounts this teaching of Jesus:

> He said to his disciples, "Things that cause sin will inevitably occur, but woe to the person through whom they occur. It would be better for him if a millstone were put around his neck and he be thrown into the sea than for him to cause one of these little ones to sin. Be on your guard! If your brother sins, rebuke him; and if he repents, forgive him. And if he wrongs you seven times in one day and returns to you seven times saying, 'I am sorry,' you should forgive him."
>
> Luke 17:1–4

We are called to be forgiving, but we are called to stand up for the truth and not water it down because it is difficult to accept.

We must have the proper disposition when we try to offer direction to others. We must remember the concept of Socratic irony and realize that we will only act wisely when we admit we are not wise. We may have a good path, but we need to keep searching to know if there is one even better. But even more importantly, we need to be humble. We need to admit to others that even though we think we have found the correct path, it will not always be easy to stay on that path. We will fall and stray because of our weakness, not because of our intentions. Only in humility can we ask others to follow what we say and not what we do; they will be able to excuse what otherwise would seem to be hypocrisy.

People will criticize us if we judge them, and rightfully so, because there is only one judge, and that is God. Confusion sets in, however, when people conclude that God will not judge them either. In our Christian faith, there are many who want to focus only on Jesus' gospel message of love. They interpret scriptures to mean that they can do whatever they want and do not have to follow any rules or commandments as long as they having loving intentions; that a loving God will not judge them and punish them. Some quote the gospel of John where Jesus said, "I did not come to condemn the world but to save the world" (John 12:47). They take this passage out of context to contend that they will not be condemned for their behavior. But we need to take a step back and look at a larger portion of the passage:

> I came into the world as light, so that everyone who believes in me might not remain in darkness. And if anyone hears my words and does not observe them, I do not condemn him, for I did not come to condemn the world but to save the world. Whoever rejects me and does not accept my words has something to judge him: the word that I spoke, it will condemn him on the last day, because I did not speak on my own, but the Father who sent me commanded me what to say and speak.
>
> John 12:46–49

Jesus does not condemn us, we condemn ourselves when we reject him and the words that he spoke at the instruction of his Father. All paths through life are not equally good. There are consequences associated with our choices.

A CHALLENGE TO BE AN ADULT

Of all the things we can do to guide others, the first and greatest is to teach through our actions that we believe that there is a God who loves us and who wants us to be in heaven with him for eternity. This is the starting point, because without an acceptance that there is a final destination that is worth pursuing, offering direction along the way will be meaningless. For Christians, we look at what Jesus taught in his Sermon on the Mount. He gives us the Beatitudes for guidance and tells us that putting them into action will not be easy, but that the reward will be great in heaven.

Our belief in heaven is best demonstrated by where we put our priorities in life. The sacrifices that we willingly make on our own journeys will be an example to others that we trust in something greater when our sojourning is over. We must not be afraid to let others know that we believe and trust in God, even if it leads to persecution. And we must pray to God for strength and wisdom along our journey. We must stay close to God and ask for his help and assistance because we know we cannot walk the journey alone. We must strive for holiness and be people of peace and joy so that others will want to travel with us.

We must be willing to act like adults in a society where many would rather act like teenagers and then hope and pray that we can be a positive influence, that we can be good role models. Only in this way will our society break out of its adolescence. We must be seen as tour guides who can be trusted because of our honesty, our lack of self-interest, and our knowledge. We must be seen as philosophers who pursue wisdom and truth about what we ought to do, even when that truth may not be convenient. We must be seen as independent and confident in what we believe, not anxious to take up sides and to polarize. We must be seen as peacemakers who ask questions to determine the best way to go and not to antagonize and trap.

We must not despair even when things look bleak. If our society and civilization fail as many portend, those that find themselves under water will be looking for submarine captains to help steer the ship until it resurfaces. They will no longer look to those who act like children and teenagers to be their leaders; they will humbly look to those who act like adults. Keep your vision clear, even if you need to use a periscope.

A FINAL THOUGHT ON ABORTION

Smoking was once marketed by the tobacco industry as the fashionable thing to do; it was sexy, it was cool. Early marketing appeals were made to women based on smoking's ability to help them control their weight and maintain their figure. And it was macho; we had Joe Kool and the Marlboro Man. Hollywood celebrities portrayed the glamour of smoking while the risks were kept hidden or minimized by the tobacco industry. Our government provided subsidies to tobacco growers. But how quickly our society has changed. I now see smokers relegated to standing in the cold outside of office buildings, usually out back by the loading dock. Even our president has to sneak a cigarette off camera because he is ashamed of his inability to break the habit. Smoking is no longer cool; those that smoke are outcasts, no longer tolerated by a polite society. The government sues and fines the cigarette industry that distributes what is now considered to be an immoral and dangerous product. Insurance companies do not condemn smokers but give them counsel and medical assistance to change their behaviors. We have come to know the truth about the health risks of smoking. Our vision has been cleared.

I am hopeful and confident that our society will ultimately also perceive the evil and immorality of abortion; that the light will shine through to clear our vision on this subject as well. Our government now subsidizes Planned Parenthood, the leading abortion provider in our country. Will it one day sue them and hold them accountable for the damage they have done? Will the Hollywood celebrities and Washington politicians who now fight for reproductive rights become tomorrow's advocates for the unborn children? Will insurance companies and government agencies counsel those with unwanted pregnancies and provide assistance to pursue morally acceptable choices? Laws are important, but changing hearts and opinions comes first. Before those that promote a culture of life can make progress on influencing our current society, they must make the truth about abortion and other life issues clearly known. Abortion must be seen as contrary to the *Tao;* it must become socially unacceptable. And then the truth will set us free to do what we ought to do.

CONTACT INFORMATION

If you would like to contact the author, you can e-mail him at: deaconjoe@orthoscopy.net.